The Vanguard Metho
in the Public Sector: Case Studies

D1136177

Delivering Public Services that Work

Volume 2

Edited by Charlotte Pell

Foreword by John Seddon

Published in this first edition in 2012 by:
Triarchy Press
Station Offices
Axminster
Devon. EX13 5PF
United Kingdom

+44 (0)1297 631456
info@triarchypress.com
www.triarchypress.com

A catalogue record for this book is available from the British Library.

Print ISBN: 9781908009685
Epub ISBN: 9781908009708
Kindle ISBN: 9781908009715

Contents

FOREWORD

John Seddon

I am eternally grateful to the contributors for taking the time and trouble to write about their experiences. As I read their contributions I felt, as I always do when I visit people who are employing these ideas, inspired and energised. It contrasts with how I always feel when I have been in Whitehall.

It is now four years since I wrote my polemic on public sector reform[1], but while we have seen many pronouncements from Whitehall about 'freedom' and 'localism'they are rarely put into practice.

Despite having to work against the grain, many more public-sector organisations are adopting the ideas I set out in that book; because they work. The case studies in this and the previous volume[2] illustrate how different the public sector can be, how much better the services become and how, paradoxically, these better services lead to much lower costs. The evidence is strong currency amongst those whose job it is to manage public-sector services but is weak currency amongst policy-makers with ideological fixations on scale, competition, commissioning and inspection, to mention just the big ones.

Yet I remain optimistic. Politicians come and go, ideologies can be blown off course by draughts of reason or competing moods but evidence, which is mounting all the time, doesn't go away.

In January 2012, David Cameron promised to rid the public sector of 'the system' that gets in the way. This collection of case studies shows that the current system still remains central to the problem and celebrates those who have fought the system and won.

---

1 Seddon, J. *Systems Thinking in the Pubic Sector*, Triarchy Press, 2008

2 Middleton,P. *Delivering Public Services that Work Volume 1*, Triarchy Press, 2010

INTRODUCTION

Chapters in **Part 1** of this book describe the application of the Vanguard Method to eight different systems: the Fire and Rescue Service, the Police, local government, the voluntary sector and the NHS. The case studies are written in the authors' own words.

Common to the case studies is the way leaders approached change from a position of knowledge about the 'what and why' of current performance including, in particular, an understanding of the demand placed on their organisation by service users.

The case studies also have the following characteristics in common:

- Massive improvement
- Released capacity and real savings

Improving service has halved the cost of stroke care in Plymouth, released police officers to deal with serious offences in Wolverhampton, saved Rugby Borough Council's planning service £168,000, significantly increased the number of businesses in Great Yarmouth producing safe food, reduced an enormous administrative burden on Staffordshire Fire and Rescue, halved the cost of advice cases in Nottingham, prevented unnecessary, unhelpful and expensive hospital treatment for vulnerable adults in Somerset and reduced the number of missing persons reports, currently costing Cheshire Police £3.8 million, by an incredible 75%. The savings to the wider public and the social benefits of these interventions are far greater than this.

Central to this success is a massive shift from the old '*de facto*' purpose to a new purpose, articulated from the perspective of the customer or public.

System	New Purpose	Old '*de facto*' Purpose
Development Control	Ensure that development is acceptable.	Meet the 8 and 13 week targets for minor and major applications.
Food Safety	Ensure food for public consumption is safe.	Meet inspection targets.

System	New Purpose	Old '*de facto*' Purpose
Police (West Midlands)	Active offender management, providing an excellent service to the public and doing the right thing.	To meet individual and sector targets.
Police (Cheshire)	Address requests for service, the needs of the public, keep the peace and protect the public.	Give a pre-determined level of service based on the categorisation of a call to comply with national inspection regimes.
Fire and Rescue	Put out fires and rescue people and do sensible things to prevent fires and other incidents occurring.	Help partners achieve their outcomes; Perform against indicator sets; Support the work of departments at headquarters; Fulfil the requirements of the National Framework.
Health and Social care	Maintain independence, and find the solutions to do the things that matter.	Meet functional targets and objectives.
AdviceUK	Help people pay their rent and Council Tax by making a decision and paying their benefit quickly.	Complete individual transactions.
Stroke Care	Optimise the care of patients of stroke from the start of symptoms back into the community and beyond.	Get it right in individual bits.

There are also significant differences between the case studies. Each case study has/or refers to a different:

- Customer/client/service-user/public
- Combination of politics and personalities
- Professional expertise
- Leadership style
- Inspection regime
- Budget

- Jargon
- Geographical boundary
- Management structure
- System archetype

Leaders in all case studies face major barriers to further improvement and savings, including:

- Central and local targets
- Compliance with central government and local organisational mandates
- Market-based competition
- Standardised processes
- IT systems
- Functional specialisms
- Risk aversion
- Data protection policies

In **Part 2** of the book are three essays on the theme of 'demand'.

The first essay, by Richard Davis, is an important piece about the most useful way to view demand. He discusses hidden demand, the role of geography in understanding demand and the problem with treating people as 'customers'.

The second essay by John Seddon is about how *not* to meet demand. He explains why mass production logic – where demand is treated as a transaction, standardised to become a commodity and then shared in an attempt to cut costs – is flawed. He concludes with advice on a better way to share services.

The purpose of my concluding afterword is to illustrate, with stories from the people on the receiving end of the services described in this book, why it is cheaper to take a 'leap of fact', understand what matters and deliver public services that work.

THE VANGUARD METHOD

The Vanguard Method is the method used by service organisations to change the design and management of work from a command-and-control to a systems approach. The Method moves organisations from the left hand column to the right hand column of this table.

Command and Control		New Thinking
Top-down, hierarchy	Perspective	Outside-in, system
Functional specialisation	Design	Demand, value and flow
Separated from work	Decision-making	Integrated with work
Output, targets, standards, activity and productivity: related to budget	Measurement	Capability, variation: related to purpose
Contractual	Attitude to customers	What matters?
Contractual	Attitude to suppliers	Co-operation and mutuality
Manage budgets and the people	Role of management	Act on the system
Control	Ethos	Learning
Reactive. Change by project/initiative	Approach to change	Adaptive, integral, emergent
Extrinsic	Motivation	Intrinsic

The Vanguard Method is a unique approach to change in that it starts with getting knowledge about the 'what and why' of current performance as a system.

The Method was originally developed by John Seddon who began his career researching the reasons why major change programmes fail. Based on what he learned, he developed this method for change, which can be described as a combination of systems thinking – how the work works – and intervention theory – how to change it. John has received numerous academic honours for his contribution to management science.

The Method provides leaders with the means to study their organisation as a system and, on the basis of the knowledge gained, to re-design their services to improve performance and drive out costs.

The Method has evolved through more than 20 years of application in the private sector and over 10 years of application in the public sector. In this time, Vanguard consultants have learnt how to help clients study the systems faster and more efficaciously, ensuring that the studying is effective for different system archetypes.

Check – Plan – Do

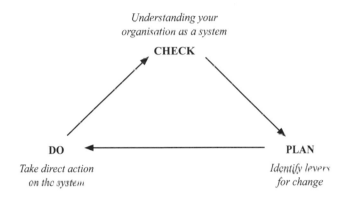

There are three steps in the Vanguard Method, known as 'Check – Plan – Do'.

In 'Check', you *get knowledge* of the 'what and why' of current performance by working through these steps (the steps for all transactional services):

- Purpose: What is the purpose of this system?
- Demand: What is the nature of customer demand?
- Capability: What is it predictably achieving?
- Flow: How does the work work?
- System Conditions: Why does the system behave this way?
- Thinking: Underlying assumptions about how the work is managed.

In 'Plan' and 'Do', you redesign the system.

A glossary of terms used is given at the end of the book.

PART ONE

1. THE NEW DEVELOPMENT CONTROL SERVICE IN RUGBY

"ABSOLUTELY BLOODY FANTASTIC"

Sean Kennedy, Change Officer, Rugby Borough Council

This case study illustrates the following:

- Flawed management thinking is the root cause of poor performance.

- Putting the staff who can solve people's problems at the first point of contact improves service and reduces cost.

- Performance indicators do not reflect the true customer experience.

- Culture change comes free with the Vanguard Method.

- Costs fall when you improve your service.

- Improvement is not a one-off activity. It's every day.

- IT should enable the process, not dictate it.

Background

Rugby Borough Council (RBC) is a rural area covering 357 square kilometres, encompassing the town of Rugby (population approximately 63,000), together with 41 parishes ranging in population from as few as 20 to nearly 3,000. The council has a total annual turnover, including housing, of about £55 million.

How we got started

Rugby Borough Council's introduction to Vanguard came when one of our strategic directors attended a talk given by John Seddon in early 2008. Although initially sceptical and defensive about John Seddon's approach, on the journey home our director had a revelation that perhaps Rugby Council too was suffering from the poor performance and hidden wastes that the Vanguard Method had exposed in other organisations.

At the time, Rugby Council was going through a period of restructuring and improvement initiatives. The Vanguard Method seemed to have the potential to provide a framework for this activity.

Later that year we arranged for the senior leadership team and two members of Cabinet, the leader and his deputy, to attend a 3-day Fundamentals course with Vanguard. This was an opportunity for the key decision-makers at the council to experience first-hand the principles and techniques associated with the Vanguard Method. The 3-day course was very successful at challenging the thinking of all involved and helped to secure the buy-in needed to progress to a full intervention.

Development Control

An intervention in the department dealing with planning applications, Development Control (DC), was initiated in early November 2008 using the Check-Plan-Do framework. This work was led by Steve Maddocks of Vanguard Consulting. The team assigned to the review was made up of the DC manager, cross-departmental staff from each stage of the flow and the two RBC Change Officers who would be trained by Vanguard to lead future interventions.

Development Control was chosen as the first intervention for a number of reasons. Primarily it was chosen because the managers and staff were ready and had an appetite for improvement but there were also known problems in the provision of service as customers complained about the poor service they received.

Development Control is a service area very much in the public eye because it can create problems for politicians and prevent investment and regeneration in the borough if the system is broken. DC had suffered from a chain of interventions to improve customer service, based around 8- and 13-week targets set at a national level. For many years the council had been paid Planning Delivery Grants to meet these targets and alongside this was a payment for e-planning. The latter part of this payment led us to force an already broken system into an electronic format dictated by an off-the-shelf product. In addition to this, in 2005 incoming telephone calls to DC were taken away from the service and transferred to a corporate contact centre.

At the start of the review the Development Control team consisted of a Development and Enforcement Manager, a Development Team Leader, 3 Principal Planning Officers, 2 Senior Planning Officers, 4 Planning

Officers, 2 Enforcement Officers, a Section 106 Officer, a Technical Support Team Leader and 7 Technical Support Officers.

Check

The purpose of Development Control in customer terms was agreed as follows:

To ensure that development is acceptable

Evidence gathered during 'Check', however, indicated that the service was actually run with a different implicit purpose:

Meet the 8- or 13-week target for minor and major applications

This was most clearly shown in the measures used, the flow of work and the way the service was managed.

How well were we meeting purpose?

Analysis of demand during 'Check' showed that at least 35% of the demands hitting the service were Failure Demands[3]. The most common demands recorded during 'Check' were:

Value (total 47%):

I would like to comment on an application, condition or conservation area appraisal	17%
I'd like to discuss my proposal / Do I need planning permission? (1st contact)	9%
Can I see / have historical planning information?	8%
Can I see plans / have information about a current application?	7%
Other	6%

Failure (total 35%):

Can I speak to…(2nd, 3rd, 4th... contact)	8%
I'd like to discuss my proposal / Do I need planning permission? (2nd or subsequent contact)	7%
I would like a progress update	6%
You've asked me for more information on my current application, here it is	4%
Here is my application (after multiple contacts prior to submission)	4%
I have already contacted you and I am still waiting for a response	4%
Other	2%

---

3 See the Glossary for this and other Vanguard Method terms.

The remaining 18% of demand was deemed unclassifiable by the team.

A common finding of all our work with Vanguard has been that the performance indicators used by our services do not reflect the true customer experience.

In the case of DC, national indicators set by central government measure the percentage of applications decided within the 8-week target date (for so called 'minor' and 'other' applications) and within the 13-week target date (for 'major' applications). At the time of 'Check' our performance in these terms, while not outstanding, was certainly above the targets and there was no apparent cause for alarm. Using measures derived from the customer's perspective, however, we uncovered a different story.

The measure charted here is the true end-to-end (E2E) time from the customer's point of view, i.e. from the date of the initial application to the date when they could actually start building. The data shows individual cases selected randomly over a period of 3 years and tells us that the average time taken to process applications in a true end-to-end way during this period was a staggering 146 days, with an upper control limit (UCL) of 515 days. More enlightening perhaps was the recognition that the most common time taken (the mode) was exactly 56 days, which equates to the 8-week government target.

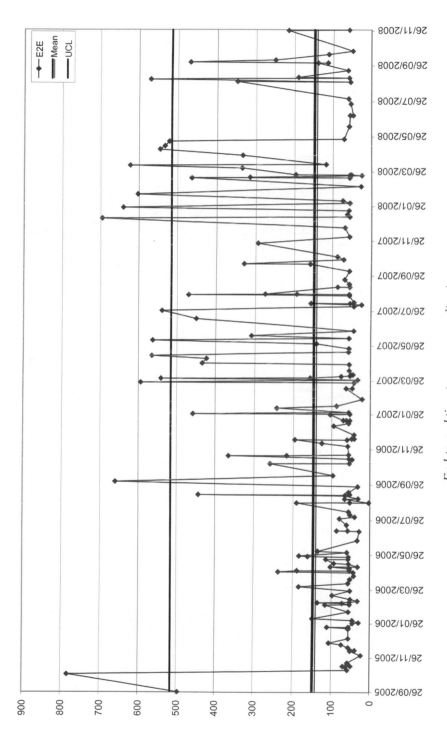

End-to-end time to process applications

Mean = 146 days   Upper Control Limit (UCL) = 515 days

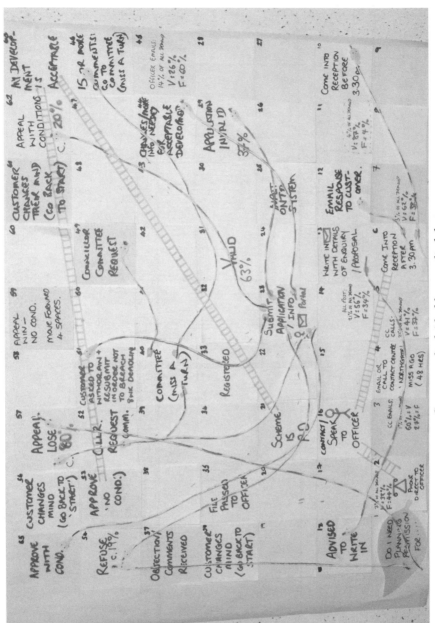

*Customers had 4 ladders to climb but
15 snakes to slide down*

When studying the flow of work through the planning system the team was surprised by the number of times the customer's journey would loop back to repeat a previous stage. It was often a case of one step forward and three steps back.

The route through the process was so repetitive and loaded with pitfalls that the team actually decided to represent the customer journey as a large "snakes and ladders" board. Unfortunately for our customers there were only four ladders to climb but fifteen snakes to slide down!

Typical customer experience

From the evidence we had gathered in 'Check' it was easy to see from a customer's point of view some of the problems associated with a typical journey through our planning service:

- If I come into reception outside of the 'consultation period' I'm told to go home and come back again after 3.30pm.

- When I see a planning officer in reception I am asked to go home and put everything I have already asked them in writing.

- I can't telephone a planning officer directly; I have to phone a call centre that can't help me. The call centre passes my message on and tells me to wait up to 48hrs for a response; this isn't helpful especially when I don't hear back from anyone even after 48hrs.

- It can take several weeks just for my planning application to be registered.

- If my application has not been decided and the 8-week deadline is approaching I am asked to withdraw it and resubmit a 'free' one.

- I am often not informed when my neighbour is planning to build something.

- Things take such a long time and it costs me and my client money.

- When I obtain planning permission it is only conditional and you still want me to submit additional details before I can commence building work.

Staff experience

Questionnaires were given to all the Development Control staff during 'Check' to help us understand what the system was like for the people working within it. A representative selection of answers is given below:

What's it like to work here?

- "Friendly and knowledgeable staff but it can be chaotic and stressful to work here"
- "The team are great but the atmosphere is very stressful"
- "I have to jump from priority to priority"
- "Managers change their mind about what is a priority"
- "I am not free to make any decisions"
- "Unnecessary meetings waste my time"
- "Sometimes policies and procedures restrict process"

What does your manager focus on?

- "Manager is focused on planning committees"
- "Manager focuses on major applications"
- "Managers focus on requests from senior leaders"
- "Manager focuses on targets"
- "Manager focuses on checking and signing-off docs and committee reports"
- "Who is my boss?!"

How does your manager spend their time?

- "Managers spend their time in meetings"
- "All planning applications have to be signed off by senior managers"

How do you know if you're doing a good job?

- "I know that I'm doing a good job if the work is done within the various time constraints"
- "If we get no complaints we assume we've done a good job"

- "I judge the performance of my team through how many applications they get through in a week and if the in-tray is empty"

Why was our system performing like this?

System conditions are the constraints inherent in the design of the work that cause waste. Through our work in Development Control we found the following key conditions were driving waste into our system.

- *Government targets were used to manage and prioritise the work.* This meant that focus was placed on applications that had yet to miss the target to the detriment of those that had already breached it. It also meant that planning officers followed two common practices used nationwide to 'cheat' the target. The first was to 'deal with' an application about to pass the target date by telling the customer it will not be approved in its current state but if they want to withdraw the application and submit a new one we can work with them to make sure this new one is acceptable. The second way to ensure the target date was met was to add multiple conditions to a decision notice which effectively meant that the customer still had work to do before they could gain permission to build.

- *The IT system dictated the process and was full of wasteful steps.* The flow map of the processes involved with feeding data into IT systems filled up entire walls. This was such an onerous part of the work that much of it was carried out by a dedicated team of admin staff.

- *All of the phone calls to the service were handled by a central call centre.* The call centre rarely transferred calls directly to planning officers, instead messages were sent as 'service request' emails to which the officers had up to 48 hours to respond according to their service standards.

- *Customers could only come into reception to see a planning officer from 3:30 to 5:00pm.* In addition to this limitation, we found through listening to the demand on reception that only simple queries were dealt with at this first point of contact. Any question that was non-trivial would be asked for in writing before a considered response would be given.

- *The procedures stated – "Get everything in writing".* The desire to create a papertrail extended to telephone calls as well as face-to-face enquiries.

Flawed thinking

The next step was to understand the management thinking and assumptions that had led to our system operating in this way.

The team explored why the system conditions in this service existed and came up with several key drivers based on the assumptions and thinking that operate at management level and across the organisation:

- Planners are considered expensive and scarce so should be protected from wasting time talking to the customer or performing "non-professional" activities.

- We think that IT will improve any process and solve any problem.

- We assume that splitting up the work and passing it through functional departments is the cheapest and most efficient way to design services.

- We think that government targets tell us how well we're doing and we concentrate on meeting their targets because if we don't we won't receive a Planning Delivery Grant.

- We believe that managers should constantly check the work of their team as this will prevent errors and improve quality.

The beauty of the Vanguard Method is that by this stage the whole team could see how flawed this thinking was. The findings of 'Check' proved that, rather than driving a more effective and efficient service, this erroneous thinking was a direct cause of the poor performance we had seen.

Redesign

The redesign of Development Control began in January 2009. The first step was for the team to define new principles to guide their work. At this stage there was a shared, clear and evidenced understanding that the way we think about work and the underlying assumptions made were driving the system and thus the performance. By challenging the thinking that led us to our current position we were able to define new principles for working that could then be used and tested as we redesigned the work in a new way.

New principles

The new principles the team came up with were:

- Focus on ensuring development is acceptable (achieving our purpose)
- Minimise hand-offs
- Minimise checks
- Eliminate errors
- Keep customers informed
- Ensure information given by customers is accurate and sufficient for purpose
- Ensure the council gives accurate information
- IT should help the process not lead it
- Changes and decisions should be based on fact and knowledge
- Measures should be based on purpose
- Understand causes of variation and improve consistency
- Work consistently from a set of principles, not 'set in stone' procedures. Review them regularly.
- Seek to answer demand at first contact

The team identified the value steps needed to meet purpose for the customer:

Can I build x?

Get all necessary information and data (including site visit)

Make decision

The redesign of Development Control was driven by the aim of only doing the value steps in the process using these new principles of working derived from the findings of 'Check'.

New features

The main features of the redesigned service are:

- Planning officers are now the first point of contact for customers and they deal with all aspects of an application from start to finish (including pre-app advice and all administrative work).

- Telephone calls for the service are no longer taken by the council's call centre but are routed straight through to the team.

- Work is no longer allocated to planners by a manager; instead it is picked up as it comes in by the next available officer. Less experienced planners, should they pick up a case with elements that are unfamiliar to them, pull support from senior officers. In this way training takes place naturally on the job.

- As much work as possible is carried out on a new case immediately and without interruption. It was proved in redesign that the work flows better and achieves a fast and successful resolution if the initial work is carried out fully and correctly by an expert.

- Decision notices are no longer checked by senior managers. The onus on individual officers is to produce quality work in collaboration with their peers; the onus on managers is to ensure the system is working to achieve this.

- A new version of the IT system has been designed to help the process and minimise the amount of waste work created.

- The way customers request searches of planning history has also changed completely. Customers are no longer required to give three days notice and, instead of being handed a huge folder of previous history on a property, the RBC officers now ascertain at first contact what specific information people are looking for and then find only this and provide it to the customer. This saves enormous amounts of time and effort on the part of RBC officers and our customers who, in this instance, are mostly search agents.

Results in the 'Plan' phase were very encouraging and proved to leaders and staff that the new way of working would be better. By June 2009, when the pilot phase had been in operation for five months, the average time to complete applications came down to 45 days with an upper control limit (UCL) of 92.5 days, in comparison with the historical figures gathered in 'Check' where the average time was 146 days and the UCL 515 days. By this stage two additional planning officers had been 'rolled-in' to the new way of working and we were ready to roll-in the rest of the planning staff.

Customer feedback

Customers responded well to the new way of working and some of the comments received at the time reflect this:

> *"Thanks for your help and prompt reply"*

> *"Absolutely bloody fantastic!"*

> *"You have taken me by surprise with the speed of your site visit ... it is usually 4 weeks minimum. I would like to add that this early site visit and communication is most appreciated as it allows time to discuss with the client and reproduce the drawings required."*

> *"Your reply regarding _____ is clear, comprehensive and timely. Thank you very much indeed. I believe I can now save a client some money and you some further time."*

A few problems

Moving into the 'Do' phase and rolling staff into the new system didn't run as smoothly and the end-to-end measures suffered as a result. By April 2010 all of the planning staff had been rolled-in but the new system was performing very poorly in comparison to its pilot capability. End-to-end times were running at an average of 94 days with a UCL of 307 days and there was a backlog of approximately 130 pieces of work that had yet to be picked up.

Some of the key reasons identified for this degradation in performance were:

- Staff members were not rolled-in to the new system of working quickly enough, leading to decreased output from both them and their mentor as they got up to speed. This problem was exacerbated by the fact that each officer who came into the new system carried an increasingly large caseload of work with them from the old system. This meant that the time needed for them to understand the new principles and start working in the new way was prolonged.

- Managers and staff were not using the new measures regularly and consistently and therefore were not able to recognise and understand changes in the system and respond to the variation in performance in a timely manner. In addition to this, the targeted performance indicators that had been shown to have a detrimental effect on performance, and were known to drive the wrong behaviours into management and staff, were still being reported to council members.

- There was difficulty in maintaining improvement activities (known as 'Job 2') when the value work (known as 'Job 1') was taking up so much time. This created a vicious cycle.

- The new IT system took a long time to implement and bring on-line. This in turn had an impact on the workload and output of the senior planning officer tasked with managing the new IT design.

- The continued impact of the Single Status Review (the agreement brought in to address inequalities in pay and conditions among local government workers) on staff morale.

Solving problems

By the end of October 2010 the backlog of work had been eradicated. The number of new demands waiting in the in-tray now rarely gets above ten. The average end-to-end time for customers started to drop; in November 2010 it stood at 84 days. However, the average then began to rise slightly and stabilised at 85 days until the first half of 2011. At this point, we began to lose staff (for a variety of reasons) and the figure started to rise incrementally to a new average of 89.3. Although disappointing to see the figure rise, it is still much lower than the average of 146 days we saw in 'Check' and with 5 fewer planners this is a considerable achievement.

In order to help eliminate the backlog of work and bed-in the new way of working, two extra planning officers were recruited on one-year temporary contracts. This helped us smooth the transition from the old to the new system of working and should allow the team to get back to a position where 'Job 2' improvement activity can take place. Job 2 has been neglected within Development Control since the initial roll-in. This was caused in part by a natural tendency to focus on Job 1 (the value work) when the workload was piling up. Job 2 has also been given diminished focus because many in the team feel that improvement work is a one-off activity that occurred when the system was redesigned and no longer needs to take place regularly, or else it is the responsibility of managers. This indicates a problem with fully embedding the new principles into the whole team and, although attitudes are slowly changing, there is still a lot of work to be done in this area.

The great thing is that we are still receiving very positive feedback from our customers, especially from planning agents who in the past were regularly frustrated by our old ways of working. This is a sure sign that we are doing the right thing and all the effort has been worthwhile. For example:

> *"This may come as a shock to you but I felt I had to drop you a line to say how impressed I have been by the changes in the planning department. Commercial life is difficult enough at the moment so positive contributions towards job creation are especially welcome. Planner x has been very proactive on the _____ application despite the Highways Agency making life virtually impossible; please pass on our thanks for his help. The new access arrangements with duty planners and short notice appointments have been well received. We bought a unit in _____ Road for a client and needed to get consent for an extension, Planner y was particularly helpful and it has enabled us to get an application in within a few days of the meeting. I appreciate that the changes may have been painful but to overcome previous perceptions is no mean feat. Keep up the good work."*

There has also been an enormous reduction in official complaints about the service. This calendar year complaints have dropped to an average of 2 per quarter from the previous average of 7 per quarter.

New measures

One of the most significant changes made at Rugby Council is the re-education of councillors in the adoption of more useful measures. The performance indicator targets are no longer captured or reported to council and have been replaced with our customer-related measures that, importantly, are not used as targets. This is a major achievement for the staff at RBC as it removes, at its root, one of the main causes of waste and failure seen in the old planning system.

Staff feedback

Anna Rose, Head of Planning and Culture:

> *"As a Head of Service I find that I now know a lot more about the system of work in Development Control. I no longer view only the headline figures but instead I understand the nature of the work coming in and how well we are dealing with that demand. I have*

found that my natural management style fits really well with the new way of working. I naturally ask my teams how they are getting on and what they feel the issues are but now I know what questions to ask to get the information I need to allow improvements to happen. I have learnt how to empower people without leaving them feeling open to blame and how to enable change without directing it. I have also learnt when to take control and when to let others lead instead."

Nick Freer, Development & Enforcement Manager:

"Operating using the new thinking has had a fundamental impact on the culture of the Development Management Team and the way it operates. Every member of the team is now much more customer-focused rather than just target-driven. Planners are more focused on resolving issues for customers rather than giving decisions by set deadlines and operate in a much calmer manner. The new way of working is showing a significant decrease in the time taken to fully answer all of the demands we receive, not just planning applications, and therefore gives a much better service across the broad spectrum of demands that we receive. In addition, the number of formal complaints received against the service, previously accepted as part of the territory in development control, has significantly fallen. We have also nurtured a paradigm/culture of continuous improvement within the team which puts us in a much better position to adapt to change as well as improve the system we operate in.

The way we now operate gives greater responsibility to planning officers, particularly more junior planners, and this in turn develops their professional abilities at a far greater pace than in the previous system. Consequently our capabilities as a team have improved at a faster rate too. If I'm honest I was very reticent to let go of the controls and not have every decision and report checked by my most senior planners but to date, my concerns have proved false. If you have the right calibre of officer and you show that you trust their judgement, my experience is that they will step up to the mark and exercise the levels of professionalism, responsibility and accuracy you could wish for. The transition has not been easy but the way we operate now is a much more efficient and effective way of focusing what resources we have to meet the array of demands that we receive.

This journey has taught me how important it is to continuously monitor work and how it is undertaken and identify and remove blockages/ problems/waste in the system in an ongoing and incremental manner alongside encouraging individual officers to identify and resolve their own system problems. I've recognised the importance of getting accurate data on issues before seeking to introduce change and when change is necessary, to introduce it as short term, incremental, experiments rather than 'sea change' actions that are set in stone. I've also had to be constantly on guard against the natural inclination for people (including myself) to revert to doing things the way we always used to. I find I have more time to spend with individual officers than I used to and I now recognise the importance of making the system work for the team rather than telling people what to do and when to do it."

Debra Harrison, Planning Officer:

"If I had dealt with Local Planning Applications like this when I was an agent I think life would have been a lot easier!"

Martin Needham, Planning Officer:

- *"Ownership and more responsibility of caseload is motivating.*

- *Dealing with one thing at a time helps focus on the task at hand and gets the job done properly.*

- *Greater variety of work (types of application) is leading to good experience and staff development.*

- *Opportunities to contribute ideas and help improve the system."*

Richard Holt, Principal Planning Officer:

- *"The new system results in officers being more accountable for their actions which I believe is good.*

- *The new system means less-experienced officers get the opportunity to deal with a more varied caseload and gain knowledge of other areas of planning which they may not have done at their level under the old system.*

- *Customer benefits from having single point of contact and direct telephone lines*

- *Quicker decisions, particularly for householder applications."*

Karen McCulloch, Principal Planning Officer:

- *"Applications take as long as they need, which has many advantages over the old approach of getting to 8 weeks and refusing or withdrawing.*

- *Customers know who they will be dealing with throughout the process, this is also an advantage for officers as in the previous way of working there would be cases where an officer could receive an application and find they had different views over whether it was valid, the description, the consultees, etc.*

- *A customer being able to call or see an officer whenever we are open is better for them; it also stops officers having a build-up of messages to return.*

- *Pull not push – This way of allocating work appears to reduce the pressure and stress, particularly when returning from leave, etc."*

Financial impact

We did not approach Vanguard with a view to cutting costs, however it is important to recognise that running the service in a new and better way actually costs us less money.

By radically redesigning the way Rugby Council deals with customer demands into the planning service we found we no longer had a requirement for the team of administrators who supported the planners. Five full-time posts and three part-time posts were made redundant across 2009 and 2010.

The other major outcome was the removal of telephone support from the council's call centre, this has saved the service £58,800 per annum.

The following table summarises the financial impact of using the Vanguard Method on the Development Control service.

	2008/09	2009/10	2010/11	2011/12	2012/13
Costs					
Consultancy costs	£50,306	£10,790	-	-	-
Redundancy costs		£20,248	£38,932	-	-
Temporary staff costs			£47,324	£10,097	-
Savings					
Staff savings (ongoing)		£87,041	£117,090	£119,763	£119,763
Call centre savings (ongoing)			£58,800	£58,800	£58,800
Net annual savings (current and projected)	-£50,306	£56,003	£89,634	£168,466	£178,563

Advice for those looking to use the Vanguard Method

- Start by engaging with leaders, it is vital that they understand the role they have to play

- The best way to learn is through doing and the best place to start is by learning how to view and understand your organisation as a system

- Build internal capacity to facilitate further interventions

- Work closely with support services (such as IT) and identify as early as possible the demands that will be placed on them

- Use the right data and measures to help understand and improve the work

- Develop and test a set of principles to guide the work and then use them

- Don't be afraid to experiment; mistakes are okay as long as you learn from them

Conclusion

The lessons we learnt from the Development Control review are being used not only to help us understand how to run further interventions but also to understand how the council as a whole can change in the future.

Since the intervention in Development Control, RBC has now carried out successful reviews in two further service areas: Benefits and Housing Repairs. Smaller pieces of work are also taking place in several other areas as we look to train managers and staff across the council in the new approach.

The leadership team is starting to learn what changes need to happen at a corporate level based on all the work that has taken place. It is doing this by understanding common themes that have emerged from each of the interventions. This should allow us to remove, organisationally, the key system conditions that drive waste and this in turn will make further improvements to a wider range of services easier.

This is a transitional time for RBC as we move towards our goal of changing the way we think and operate organisation-wide while at the same time coping with the implications of budgetary cuts. With the current financial pressures that all public sector organisations are under we feel that changing our thinking using the Vanguard Method is the right way to improve the quality and efficiency of our services instead of taking the 'slash and burn' approach that we might otherwise have adopted.

About the author

Sean Kennedy
Change Officer, Business Improvement Team.
Rugby Borough Council.
Tel: 01788 533 533 (ask for Doug Jones)

Sean started his employment at Rugby Borough Council in May 2008, in a role created specifically to facilitate systems thinking interventions within the council. Since submitting this case study he has returned to the private sector where he works as an internal consultant for a FTSE100 company.

2. FOOD SAFETY IN GREAT YARMOUTH

AN ADULT CONVERSATION

Kate Watts, Environmental Health Services Manager

This case study illustrates the following:

- A productive role for managers is to work with the team to fix problems and act on the system.

- In a regulatory system, not all risks are equal when understood in context. Concentrate resources on real risk.

- Business operatives want to do the right thing. Environmental Health Officers want to do a good job. But the system design and conventional thinking about what motivates people prevented them from doing so. Now the system enables the professionals to work with businesses to make food safe.

- Targets incentivise staff to cheat and avoid work that doesn't help them meet the target.

- Building and maintaining relationships with customers in a regulatory system is more likely to achieve purpose than sending letters.

- A one-size-fits-all approach to regulation does not gain the respect of customers who have a variety of contexts and needs.

- Practical demonstrations that show people how to do something are often more effective than simply telling someone something is wrong.

Background

Great Yarmouth is the premier tourist destination in Norfolk. Visitors and residents alike are fed by a large number of shops, cafés, restaurants, pubs, B&Bs, hotels and takeaways.

This case study is about Food Safety, the service responsible for carrying out food safety inspections, enforcing food safety law, handling complaints from the public and running the food safety star award scheme.

Over the years, we had found our capacity to deal with proactive work decreased as reactive workloads increased. However, it was clear that, despite repeated requests for help, we would never be given any extra staff particularly in the wake of the financial cuts to local authorities.

So where did the Vanguard Method come in? Vanguard came in to run a three days 'Fundamentals' course for managers across the council. This showed us the potential of the method. In the case of Environmental Health, it illustrated that it might be possible to return to our true purpose without having to find additional resources.

Check

In March 2010, a team of four Environmental Health staff and one Vanguard Consultant started to apply the Vanguard Method to Food Safety. Our first task was to find out how the service was broken and then identify the management thinking responsible. Although we knew there were problems, we had never been given the tools or time to be able to identify what and why.

During 'Check', we identified demands from food businesses, members of the public and the Food Standards Agency. We then explored each demand further hoping that this would help us determine an overall purpose for Food Safety.

When we looked at the demands from an outside-in perspective, we found that members of the public often just wanted to tell us they had seen something that "didn't look right" in a food establishment. We learnt that they expected us, as the professionals, to do something about it. We found that this demand did not require feedback unless the person complaining had been harmed or perceived that they had been harmed. In the old system, we wasted time struggling to return calls from people who did not actually want further contact from us.

On closer inspection of the demand, we discovered that the majority of complaints were indicators of poor or stretched management in a food business. When we started to treat complaints as indicators, we uncovered failings in food safety management by looking at that business as a whole instead of just focusing on the complaint.

We learnt that food businesses wanted advice and guidance, and to know that they were meeting the expectations of the Environmental Health Department. We also discovered food businesses actually wanted face-to-face contact from officers. Many said this should be done more often and even businesses with a poor compliance history expressed the same view.

In the old system only one fifth of food businesses were revisited by us following an inspection. In letters we sent to them after a visit, we often said "a revisit may take place in the next few months to check compliance with this letter". However, when we listened to businesses, they said all they wanted was to show us what they had done as a result of their previous inspection. They actually wanted us to visit them again. They also talked about their interpretation of the last inspection and what it covered. Officers were surprised about some of the aspects that were being recalled, many not directly important to food safety.

Legislation itself was an interesting demand and perhaps, with hindsight, it is not actually a demand on the system. However, the initial assumption of the team was that the food safety service was there to ensure compliance with legislation and that, by doing so, food businesses would be safe. We complied through carrying out a regime of proactive inspections. In the old system, there were approximately 450 inspections overdue out of a total of 1,432 food businesses in the Borough.

Inspections themselves were cyclical in nature and required businesses to be re-inspected on a risk-rated basis. So we knew that, unless a business closed, any new system would have to take this into account.

After much debate and analysis of these demands the purpose of the system was determined:

To ensure food for public consumption is safe

This newly defined purpose allowed the team to reflect on a personal level why they originally chose to join the profession of Environmental Health. They generally said that they joined to protect people and make a difference.

But had we been achieving this purpose? And if we had, how much waste had we been creating in doing so? Looking at measures in the old system, we were not able to determine whether we had either positively or negatively affected the safety of food businesses. We simply didn't know.

Mapping the flow

Mapping the flow of a typical proactive food safety inspection revealed a total of 184 steps. Of these 184 steps, 116 came about because the Environmental Health Officer had to return to the office to 'sign off' a piece of work, handing it to a total of 11 different sections just so a letter could be produced and sent to the food business in question. The team quickly realised how much work it was creating for others in the organisation. It really demonstrated the importance of looking at a system 'end-to-end'.

In the old system, officers were given inspection targets to achieve on a monthly basis, driven by their managers and ultimately by the Food Standards Agency. We found 'cheats' where work had been double entered onto computer systems so that it could be counted twice, thereby helping officers meet inspection targets. We also avoided putting new premises onto the system because they added to the heavy backlog of inspections that needed to be done. However, with fresh eyes it was clear to see that the old system was driving this behaviour because it focused purely on the numbers.

At the end of 'Check' the old system was summarised, and it was easy to see what had driven this system and the thinking behind it. It was also clear that our thinking needed to change so that we could become far more capable of delivering its newly identified purpose.

Redesign

Equipped only with principles, the team visited a food business with no inspection aids. At this stage, we did not understand why we were experimenting with the actual inspection visit itself, because we were so sure that 'Check' had not shown this part of our work to be wasteful.

Returning from the first experimental visit, we learned so much more than we would have done on a normal visit. We found that bad food hygiene practices had been adopted and ingrained by the operator since our last visit and now a lack of money stood in the way of making changes that would help them produce safe food for their customers. We learned it would have been much more beneficial if we had visited when the business changed hands over a year ago, rather than waiting for the routine inspection date to come up on the system.

Armed with this information, the team carefully considered how we could work with this business to help them make the changes required while considering some of the constraints at the same time.

Simply by booking a revisit and spending time with this operator, showing him what he needed to do to make safe food through practical hand wash demonstrations and food sampling, he engaged with us and put things right to make his food safe.

So, although we had argued that inspection was the wrong place to start in terms of experimentation, we found that by inspecting against a purpose, and finding out what matters to the business during this process, we were then able to help it achieve safe practice.

As we visited more businesses we learnt many more important lessons. We learnt that a one-size-fits-all approach to assessing a food business in the new system was not going to work. Unsafe businesses required a more rigorous assessment than those that were already producing safe food. Businesses already producing safe food could be assessed through simple verification checks, sampling visits and even over the phone when they only handled pre-packed, low-risk foods.

We learned that unsafe businesses did not always realise how poor they were. In the old system, unless we closed a business down, the food business operator was left with a feeling that they must be satisfactory. This was further compounded by the star rating scheme we used - a business with one star left them feeling they had achieved something. But as inspectors we knew that a one-star rating meant that the level of food hygiene was not good.

Nevertheless it was clear that businesses did want some kind of recognition if everything was satisfactory at the time of our visit. This continues to be something we are looking into as part of the new system.

Practical demonstrations

During experimentation we started to show the bad businesses how unsafe they were. We used techniques ranging from simply discussing what they were doing in terms of real risk and potential harm to their customers, to totalling up maximum fines and showing the business on a graph where it ranked in terms of other businesses in the Borough. The impact of this moved some business operators to tears. It also facilitated a significant change in those people, some of whom previously paid little attention to what we were asking them to deliver.

We also learnt that rather than simply telling a business something was wrong, practical demonstrations engaged them in a much more positive way. For example, we showed them how to wash their hands, use UV gel and light, how to sample food, take protein swab samples and reorganise safe food storage in fridges.

By actually booking a date and time for a revisit at the end of the initial assessment, much of the work we were asking a business to complete was being achieved by our return visit, even when we weren't asking for it to be done by this date.

In the old system, letters were the focus of our work after an inspection. But it became apparent that in most instances the information we gave at the time, backed up in writing on site, was the most important for the business. This is the information they used, not a letter that often took up to two weeks to arrive.

Not all risks are equal

During experimentation the team questioned the role of legislation in our new system. Food safety is governed by many pieces of legislation dictating what a food business needs to do in order to comply. The team found that legislation had been devised as a sound basis for any food business to follow to help them produce safe food. As inspectors in the old system we felt our role was to ensure that a business fully complied with all legislation. However we did not differentiate between real and perceived risks.

Equal weighting was given to each individual requirement when some, in certain circumstances, posed a direct risk to food safety, whilst others didn't.

For example, we found that a food business operator who was extremely knowledgeable about food safety, fully engaged with us when discussing the location of a new wash hand basin. However, when we mentioned a cracked shelf in a fridge, he became agitated that we were asking for a repair in an area that posed little risk (he was only storing drinks cans in there). This showed that in the old system we placed equal importance upon two separate legislative breaches when in reality only one posed a risk to food safety.

'Unsafes' and legislative breaches

The team then began to experiment with splitting breaches into the categories of 'unsafes' and legislative breaches. Significant weighting would be given to any breaches found to be in the unsafe category because if they were not addressed, there would be a real risk to food safety.

We also told food business operators about other legislative breaches and we gave them advice on how to correct these, but we left them to decide themselves when to put these things right. At the same time, we explained that if one of the legislative breaches got worse or something changed in the business, we would return to make sure they put them right.

When officers explained this difference to businesses they began to have what we now see as being an "adult conversation" with the operator. We had learnt through this process that food business operators did not set out with an intention to harm anyone and, by clearly showing them where they could make the biggest difference, they became empowered to make the changes that really mattered.

Helping to make food businesses safe

As experimentation developed, our new system began to take shape. What had once been inspections are now assessments. If a business is found to be unsafe after an assessment we deliver any number of 'make safe' visits until that business is safe and our purpose has been achieved. These 'make safes' are seen as a toolkit, with officers choosing whatever they feel would be appropriate to use for that business.

This toolkit is still developing and the team constantly analyses what worked and what didn't. It is also aware that when, on the odd occasion, a food business may choose not to work with it, the full range of enforcement powers are still available to use. However, it's worth noting that over a hundred businesses have now been inspected with this new way of working and we have not had to use enforcement once as a 'make safe' tool.

When new businesses open and complaints come in, we feed these straight into this system and they prompt an assessment. We do this because we have learnt the importance of working with a new business and developing a relationship from the start. In 'Check' we also saw that complaints could indicate general management failings. By carrying out an assessment instead of just dealing with the complaint, we are able to help the business address failings immediately. This is a much more intelligent approach than focusing only on the complaint.

Concentrating resources on real risk

If a business is safe or made safe we score it for long-term sustainability by evaluating how long we can then step away from that business while it continues to produce safe food. The score is lower if the business cooperates with us during the make safe process. This changed some areas of the traditional risk rating scoring system used previously and has allowed us to prioritise between unsafe and safe businesses and to concentrate our resources on the unsafe ones.

At this point other members of the food safety service who were not part of the initial stages of the intervention started to be rolled-in to this new way of working. They were surprised by the change in our relationship with food business operators, and the fact that so many of these businesses are putting right many things that they had never addressed before.

For example, a bakery that has been in operation for over a hundred years had struggled to comply in the old system and, historically, had a number of Hygiene Improvement Notices served on it to force compliance. In the new way of working we learnt that this business had often misunderstood what we had asked it to do, previously linking any work to a financial cost, when in fact the business needed to learn how to clean effectively. The food business operator at the bakery cannot read and write, but this had never been picked up on in previous inspections. Officers now listen in a different way and this means they find out a lot more about the business operators. In the case of the bakery, we took in photographs taken during the initial assessment to highlight problem areas rather than leaving a written list. The standard of cleaning has since dramatically improved and further checks have shown that this business is now able to maintain working in safe way.

In the old system, we were incentivised not to seek out and inspect new businesses. Finding new businesses is now a priority for officers. This change really hit home when two inspectors on the district saw a new food business and went straight to assess it, finding that another officer already in the business had got there first!

A new role for managers

Officers are not spending as much time as they used to in the office because they are writing fewer letters, completing less paperwork and only using an Excel spreadsheet to hold information on their system. This has allowed them to give businesses the face-to-face contact they asked for during 'Check'. Officers are no longer allocated work but pick their own. Managers are part of the work and no longer pay attention to targets but work with the team to fix problems and to support and develop the system.

Every day we continue to learn what we can do to achieve our purpose, getting quicker and smarter at making decisions and continuously improving the system. The learning culture is so strong that two officers decided to inspect over thirty schools, all overseen by the same external contractor, so that they can learn about how these kitchens are managed. This led to officers being able to present consistent and clear findings to the company face to face, all in one go, rather than writing separate letters throughout the year. Previously, each school was inspected as an individual unit, often with no changes being facilitated.

A new role for Environmental Health Officers

Harriet Sealey, Commercial Team Manager:

> *"I have worked within the food team at Great Yarmouth Borough Council for almost two years. I was part of the original intervention team, and I am now heavily involved in developing the new system.*
>
> *Before the intervention, I was starting to lose sight of why I had become an Environmental Health Officer. During the course of my work when interacting with businesses, I often felt that I was not helping them at all and I recall a regular feeling of embarrassment when talking to businesses about the problems that I had identified, and especially hearing businesses' complaints about the last officer never coming back to check on what they had ask the business to do. I spent a lot of my time in the office completing paperwork and not actually working in the district with the businesses. I did not feel that I had control over the work that I did and I did not feel a sense of job satisfaction, more a feeling of frustration with the bad businesses, when changes were not being achieved. There are one or two businesses that I worked with in the old system that stand out in my mind; these businesses did change their practices, and improved standards significantly, and I*

could see that I had made a big difference However, this feeling of achievement did not happen very often.

In contrast, since going through the intervention, I take a lot more pride in my work, and the sense of achievement that my time and effort has actually made a difference is now felt most days. I think this is because I can see the impact that I am having on the businesses; I have the freedom to work with them, and to build a relationship with them. I actually feel a lot more confident in my day-to-day work because I am able to use common sense when telling a business what they need to do to improve. I do not need to blindly tell them to comply with every aspect of the legislation, and I am having much more intelligent conversations with the businesses. This has removed any feeling of embarrassment that I recall feeling when working in the old system. Working in a new way I am also enjoying the freedom to explore my own ideas and the fact that I can share my successes with the rest of the team (and vice versa) so that we can work together to learn what works best with our businesses and continue to improve our service."

Adam Boggis, Environmental Health Officer:

"I have worked at Great Yarmouth Borough Council within the Health and Safety Team over the past four years and I am currently studying for my MSc in Environmental Health.

Although I don't work in the Food Safety Team I was chosen to be part of the original intervention team. To start with I wondered how I would be able to contribute in this intervention as I only had a basic understanding of food safety legislation and the way that the Food Team works, but it quickly became apparent that I would become a valuable member of the intervention team.

This basic understanding of food safety legislation and the way that the food team works led me to be inquisitive and question other team members who worked within the Food Team on why they were working in certain ways. It also gave me the opportunity to stand back and see how businesses reacted to contact with the Food Team and see and take in things that officers may have missed.

Recently I went through the 'Check' phase with the Health and Safety service and identified how different the service is compared to the Food Team. This shows that you can't just transfer over everything learned from one intervention to another.

The work in the food intervention has enabled me to carry on using some of the skills I learned within my day-to-day role within the

Health and Safety Team. I am now listening and undertaking work in a different way and feel free to experiment with my work to assist with redesigning the health and safety service.

I have seen first-hand how far the Food Team have come and I am looking forward to being part of redesigning the way the Health and Safety Team works".

New measures

To help us stay honest to our purpose, we are experimenting with a number of different measures. Given that we no longer focus on the number of inspections we carry out and instead focus on making food safe, we have a new baseline. This baseline allows us to understand how effective our different ways of helping a business are after the second visit. If a business gets worse or doesn't improve, we can try different methods. It is a much more effective method than sending letters for non-compliance. We waste no time in achieving our purpose. In the old system a high-risk business always stayed high-risk. Now more businesses are improving. This suggests that the new approach is achieving long-term sustainability and is making eating out in Great Yarmouth a safer experience for the public.

The Food Standards Agency supported us when we were experimenting and they have continued to do so as we embed our new way of working. It is great to see a regulatory body nurturing innovation and experimentation and being genuinely curious to see how things could be different.

A solid foundation

We are not there yet and still have much to do, but the foundations we have laid are solid. I am confident that as a result of the initial support from Vanguard and the dedication of the team, this new system will grow and produce the capability that the service so desperately needed.

About the author

Kate Watts
Environmental Health Service Manager
Great Yarmouth Borough Council
Telephone: 01493 846627
Email: kaw@great-yarmouth.gov.uk
Website: www.great-yarmouth.gov.uk

Kate Watts started as an Environmental Health Officer in December 2005, a career she specifically chose as she wanted to make a difference to the health and wellbeing of the general public. In 2007 she was promoted to Commercial Team Manager at Great Yarmouth Borough Council, and subsequently to Environmental Health Service Manager in 2010. She has found that by using the Vanguard Method and principles she is now able to personally deliver and guide her team to making a real difference to the community in which she and her team work.

3. WHAT WORKS AND WHAT MATTERS: WEST MIDLANDS POLICE

Inspector Simon Guilfoyle, West Midlands Police

This case study illustrates the following:

- When you are the management it is your responsibility to act.

- If you do the right thing, the numbers look after themselves.

- You can release capacity by simply reversing everything that doesn't work. Take out the non-value activity. Replace it with what works, to achieve what matters.

- If the extent of what you are able to change is limited, focus on what you can control. Take unilateral action.

- Be adaptable and flexible when carrying out 'Check'. If embedded experts have an acute understanding of the issues, it doesn't have to take weeks or months.

- Trust what members of the public are telling you. Listen to what matters to them and design your organisation to deliver it.

Introduction

Front-line bobbies know what works. Some of the best ideas about effective working practices come from the 'shop floor', and the police service is no different. The people who do the work understand it better than anyone else. It follows that they also know what doesn't work, no matter how vigorously it is imposed by management. Likewise, members of the public who call the police following an incident usually have an idea about what outcome they would like to see as a result of police intervention. They know what is important to them, and this can be as straightforward as, "please deal with my problem quickly and professionally and keep me updated".

It therefore follows that our organisational systems and structures should be geared towards achieving what matters to the public by applying what works. Although I am now an Inspector, I still proudly class myself as front-line, having spent all of my service in uniform and at the 'sharp end'. This means I have never lost my instinct for what works on the ground and, when combined with an appreciation of what matters to the public, the result can be a powerful antidote to prescriptive one-size-fits-all doctrine and inflexible operating models. The vehicle for achieving this is the application of a systems approach and organisational trust.

I joined West Midlands Police in 1995 and spent nine years as a response PC before going for promotion. Having never heard of systems thinking at that time I instinctively knew that some of the things we did were counterproductive, but couldn't understand or articulate why. Examples included set individual targets, such as to make three arrests or detect three crimes per month, or having to complete disproportionate amounts of paperwork for extremely low-level incidents.

Bizarrely, some of these very incidents involved making arrests against the explicit wishes of the caller, who often just wanted advice or for an officer to have a word with the other party. The reason this happened was to ensure compliance with strict recording procedure, as well as the need to meet performance targets for arrests and detections. Effectively, this meant that victims' wishes were overridden by internal organisational requirements and that victims were being subjected to a disproportionate and unhelpful response to their call for help. It also ensured that waste was driven into the system. The approach did not work and the outcome was not in line with what mattered to the victim.

Now that I have an understanding of the systems approach and am familiar with much of the literature that examines the unintended effects of target-driven performance management, I understand why what I was expected to do as a Police Constable in the 1990s was neither correct nor beneficial to the public. This understanding has also generated an impetus to make a difference by redesigning policing systems that enhance efficiency and deliver an improved service to the public; in other words, applying what works to achieve what *matters*.

The way we were

In October 2010 I was posted as the Sector Inspector for the North East Sector of Wolverhampton Local Policing Unit. My role involves managing seven neighbourhood policing teams, based at four separate police stations with approximately seventy staff in total, as well as coordinating a range of partnership activity. The sector covers approximately one third of Wolverhampton, and incorporates a number of challenging and diverse areas. The teams are responsible for investigating crime and dealing with anti-social behaviour, as well as managing offenders, providing targeted patrols, and combating emerging crime patterns. It has always been a particularly busy sector and, historically, the officers based there have been faced with a raft of competing priorities.

From the outset, it was apparent that there was a strong culture of 'reporting back' large amounts of information on team activity to sector management, as well as a heavy focus on control through performance targets. Teams often tended to work in 'silos', concentrating on their own beats and therefore losing sight of the bigger picture of cross-border sector criminality. Part of this was due to the disparate structure of the sector, with the seven teams being spread out between four bases, but I also developed an early sense that one of the other main barriers was cultural.

The prevailing culture in the sector at that time was like that of many hierarchical command and control organisations, and this had directly influenced the operating system. The culture and structure of the sector was excessively centralised, with limited authority being devolved to the team sergeants. This extended to examples of centralised controls, such as team sergeants not being permitted to authorise overtime for members of their own teams. Sergeants told me they felt disempowered and it was evident that the policy of centralising control had restricted the vital component of local ownership. It was also standard practice for routine supervisory activity to be subject to additional layers of checking and control by sector management, resulting in duplication, disempowerment and delays.

This culture discouraged decision-making, further disempowering front-line officers and at times supplanting proportionate risk-management with risk aversion. Aside from the range of well-documented perverse incentives and behaviours that result from this style of management, this approach also caused a distorted picture of operational activity. Priorities and daily activity were skewed by the requirement to meet performance targets, and this had an adverse affect on the cultivation of professional judgement amongst sector staff. Individual officers were the subject of performance targets, and the result of this was that achieving numerical targets often became the *de facto* purpose for much sector activity. Ironically, the achievement of targets did not necessarily correlate with what mattered to the public or what was the right thing to do.

The usefulness of available performance data was therefore significantly diminished, and this rendered interpretation of the system impossible. Managing by targets had not only built in poorer service delivery but also caused all statistical regularity to collapse. These features had resulted in processes that were burdensome and inefficient, and this had the ultimate effect of building in waste activity and rendering service delivery sub-optimal. There was also confusion about priorities and, as local policies had initiated inefficient processes, this then generated unnecessary bureaucracy and data collection. The result was that officers spent a significant proportion of their time engaged in non-value activity, which affected their ability to respond to crime, anti-social behaviour and matters of community concern; this was reflected in a relatively high crime rate.

Taken together these factors had a significant impact on operational capacity, resulting in officers carrying the highest proportion of ongoing investigations amongst any of the sectors at Wolverhampton. Although other sectors faced similar challenges, the intensity of the management style on the North East sector, coupled with its relatively high rate of demand, had disproportionately affected officers' workloads. This had become a vicious circle, as the inbuilt non-value activity prevented them from efficiently managing their existing workload, resulting in an impaired turnover rate and slower resolution for victims of crime. It also meant that the volume of ongoing investigations gradually increased and further limited officers' ability to close cases.

A further direct effect of this inertia was evident on the sector's list of outstanding offenders. Whenever someone breaches their licence conditions following release from prison, police are notified that they are subject to a prison recall and must be arrested. In the same way, when an offender has breached court bail conditions, or becomes wanted on warrant, the police are informed and that person becomes liable to arrest. Furthermore, when an offender has failed to attend a mandatory drug assessment following a positive drugs test in custody, the police are notified and that person is subject to arrest. In all cases, this populates a sector-level list of 'wanted' persons.

Before October 2010, officers were so stretched in trying to manage their existing workload that this list grew and grew, without any realistic prospect of bringing it under control. By the very nature of the people on the list, it is reasonable to suspect that some were responsible for committing further crime, which generated more ongoing investigations for sector officers. It was relatively obvious that by concentrating efforts on locating and arresting the outstanding offenders on this list, the number of suspects currently 'at large' would decrease, meaning some crimes could be prevented. The result of fewer outstanding offenders committing less crime would be that officers' existing workload might reduce and capacity would be created, thereby enabling effective management of new cases of wanted persons.

The issues with the outstanding offenders' list represented a symptom indicative of the problems faced on the sector at that time.

Why? Why? Why?

So, did all these ills occur because sector officers were bad people? Of course not. Was it the fault of my predecessor? Not really. He was just doing what was the norm up to that point. His predecessor also probably just did what was the norm up the point he moved on. And so on. The issue was a cultural and systemic one, and nothing to do with personalities.

Not blaming the staff was a good starting point; indeed many will know that Deming attributes about 94% of performance to the system. The workers operate within the constraints that the system imposes on them, and it is management's responsibility to improve the system. Only management can address the causes of failure, such as entrenched inefficiencies, waste activity and control through arbitrary numerical targets. Upon taking over the sector, I was the management – therefore it became my responsibility to act. There was no point blaming the workers. It was clear that impaired sector activity was caused by the system, and this was therefore the place to start looking for answers.

Fixing the system, taking back the streets

The first stage of improving the system was to gain an appreciation of the current state of affairs. This did not take long, and involved a speedy analysis of existing processes, workload and culture. Being a front-line operational officer I had the advantage of understanding the issues and processes already, and I was quickly able to assess local nuances through face-to-face interaction with sector officers. I believe it is important to understand local context, as well as to be adaptable and flexible when conducting 'Check'. If embedded experts understand the issues then it isn't always necessary to review large amounts of data or conduct extensive research to identify the problems.

The next step was to provide clarity about direction, purpose and priorities. This was done on a face-to-face basis with all team sergeants, and supported by a written document that was circulated to all sector staff. The purpose of this was to demonstrate ownership and to state an intention to make a positive difference to the sector. The document acted as a kind of contract; its content clearly outlined what the sector priorities would be:

Active offender management, providing an excellent service to the public, and doing the right thing.

It also placed on record the removal of all numerical performance targets forthwith and communicated that staff could expect consistency, fairness and support.

Unnecessary procedures such as the requirement for teams to produce daily returns of their activity were also removed immediately. Fresh deployment principles were implemented, which meant that officers were able to spend more time patrolling their areas and responding to the community's needs. A strong trust-based emphasis on empowering sergeants was introduced, with a minimum amount of reporting back. Sergeants were permitted to authorise overtime for their teams, and empowered to take full control of partnership activity in their areas (previously much of this was controlled directly by the Sector Inspector). A full review was also conducted of each team's existing workload.

This review found that a large proportion of existing enquiries involved carrying out unproductive activity, such as taking statements that were of little or no evidential value. Officers reported that they had not been allowed to conclude these investigations until such tasks had been conducted, regardless of the likelihood of identifying offenders. Sergeants had not felt empowered to file the reports and were obliged to continually absorb additional enquiries, even where there were no obvious actions that would result in an offender being traced. This caused a huge backlog of work, which not only slowed officers down, but also resulted in higher-priority matters being lost in the 'noise'. This meant that inefficiency thrived and service delivery was sub-optimised.

As a result of the review, sergeants were empowered to rigorously prioritise their officers' workload and the overall volume of existing enquiries was cut by approximately one third. Officers were able to concentrate on the most important matters, resulting in a faster and more effective service to victims of crime. The sum of these immediate systemic changes was that service delivery instantly became more efficient, waste activity was significantly reduced, and additional capacity was created. Sergeants reported that they liked the responsibility of the local ownership that had been afforded them, and a tangible sense of energy and purpose was injected into sector activity. One sector sergeant described the transformation as follows:

> *"At last we are able to make a difference in areas that really matter to the public, such as locking up prolific offenders and taking drug dealers off our streets. The results speak for themselves."*

Greater cross-border cooperation was also encouraged between teams, to generate a deeper understanding of criminal activity across the sector. Key offenders were targeted consistently, with a focus on the crime types that caused greatest misery to the community. Crime data was used intelligently to assist officers in understanding patterns of offences and offender activity. The use of statistical process control (SPC) charts was encouraged as a means of understanding longer-term trends and to prevent 'knee-jerking'. League tables and individual quotas were abolished, and performance information was never used as a way to apportion blame for apparent failure, but as a constructive tool to identify where systemic improvements could be made. This encouraged an ethos of organisational learning and transparency, as well as a focus on quality instead of quantity.

The extra capacity generated as a result enabled the sector to undertake additional activity previously considered impossible due to resourcing limitations. This included the regular implementation of pre-planned operations such as the execution of warrants against drug dealers and those responsible for handling stolen property. There have also been a number of high-profile arrests of serious offenders, as well as an exponential increase in the type of policing activity that has a high impact in reducing crime and disrupting the activity of key offenders.

Intelligence-led policing tactics have been employed to address emerging crime trends, such as a series of metal thefts that occurred on one beat, leading to a sustained reduction in that crime type of almost 90%.

The increased capacity meant that officers were now able to tackle effectively the perennial issue of outstanding offenders on the 'wanted' list, with notable success. The current position is that officers promptly resolve any new/wanted offender cases, (often within hours of notification), and currently there are no such wanted persons on the sector. By taking these offenders out of circulation, it follows that they are not in a position to commit further offences.

The additional capacity generated also allowed the inception of a small proactive team, drawn from officers on the neighbourhood teams. This team came into existence at the beginning of February 2011 and focuses on serious acquisitive crime, but operates with a broad remit to "proactively target key offenders and hotspots". The ethos of the team is very much about quality over quantity, as well as tackling crime by employing disruption tactics and active offender / location management, rather than attempting to record high numbers of low-impact warrants, arrests or intelligence submissions.

The proactive team is highly integrated with the other neighbourhood teams and supports their work by providing additional resources and expertise where required. Its existence is possible because of the reduced workload and more efficient working practices now embedded within the neighbourhood teams. The officers who remain on the neighbourhood teams report that they are able to manage their current workload effectively; in other words, the creation of the proactive team has not reduced their productivity.

The proactive team has generated a large volume of self-initiated work, resulting in numerous arrests and the recovery of thousands of pounds worth of stolen property and drugs. The important factor to consider here is that every single one of these pieces of work has been conducted in addition to daily sector business. This additional activity has had a wider impact and contributed significantly to overall effective sector performance.

In summary, the changes introduced to the sector have resulted in more efficient working practices, greater cooperation between teams and improved service delivery.

Measures and results

The sector restructure occurred as a result of a unilateral attempt at improving the system in my own area, but the extent of what I was able to change was limited. It was not within my remit, for example, to introduce new measures. I was only able to remove or change systemic features that were indigenous to the sector, such as local reporting requirements, structure, and the established mode of performance management.

The North East sector is one of four sectors at Wolverhampton Local Policing Unit (LPU), which is one of ten LPUs in the West Midlands Police force area. This means that my sector is still subject to force-prescribed processes, priorities and mandates; not all of these are compatible with the systems approach I have implemented locally. In effect I have been able to change things that sit below me, but I am still subject to many of the same type of reporting requirements and organisational barriers from above that I changed or removed locally. The best I can do is to try and minimise their effects and not pass them down the line to my staff, wherever possible.

One area that I would have liked to develop, but which would require a force-level change, would be to introduce alternative measures that are designed against purpose. It was relatively straightforward to articulate what our purpose was (remember "active offender management, providing an excellent service to the public, and doing the right thing"), but less obvious how existing measures such as numbers of offences detected could be linked to this type of activity. Data generated by existing force processes do not currently feed into many of the types of measures I believe would allow us to understand the capability of our systems. This means that systemic measures such as total end-to-end time for investigations, proportion of incidents dealt with at the first point of contact, or number of hand-offs within an ongoing enquiry still remain on my wish list.

It would not have been possible to introduce such measures at a sector-level without introducing additional layers of bureaucracy and data-collection, so at present I have relied on loosely tracking the sector's crime rate as a guide to the impact of the systemic changes I introduced. The theory behind this is that, generally speaking, increased capacity should result in more opportunity to undertake the sort of policing activity that prevents crime (for example, providing an increased visible presence, or arresting offenders likely to commit further offences). When coupled with a desire to do the right thing and not chase figures for the sake of it, this should have an impact on the crime rate, although it is always going to be difficult to quantify.

The charts below show crime rates on the sector:

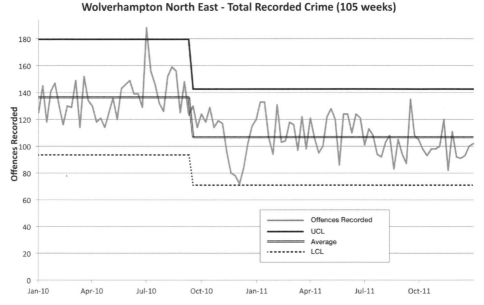

North East Sector Total Recorded Crime (weekly)
18th January 2010 – 24th October 2011

This chart shows a step change downward in the rate of total recorded crime from mid-October 2010, followed by a slight further decrease from August 2011. (The steep dip in mid-December coincided with the freezing weather and snow).

This second chart demonstrates a slight stabilisation in the rate of serious acquisitive crime (robbery, house burglary and vehicle thefts) from the beginning of October 2010, with a significant further step change following the inception of the proactive team at the start of February 2011.

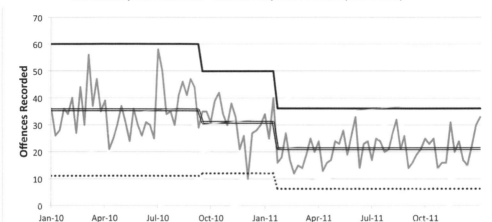

North East Sector Serious Acquisitive Crime (weekly)
18th January 2010 – 24th October 2011

At this point it is important to recognise the myriad factors affecting crime rates that are outside police control; for example, economic drivers, social deprivation, substance abuse or personal security. It would be misleading to claim a significant degree of control over crime rates, it is also important to understand that it is notoriously difficult to establish a causal link between a unit of policing activity and an eventual outcome. For this reason I cannot claim that my sector restructure is the chief reason for reduced crime rates, although I do believe it must have contributed to it, and it is certainly better than what we were doing before. The question is – was it a coincidence?

The main approach I employ to aid understanding of performance is dialogue and understanding of the narrative behind sector activity. I do not expect my sergeants to produce rows of numbers that show how many arrests their teams have recorded, for example, but I do expect them to know what is happening in their areas, and share examples of good work undertaken by their team. I also expect their teams' activity to be focused on doing the right thing and those officers do what matters to the public. Whilst difficult to quantify outputs, this new approach seems to have generated a more productive working environment and positive outlook among staff, and I frequently hear of excellent pieces of work, often from members of the public who write to me.

Another interesting side effect of the changes validates John Seddon's adage of 'If you try and manage costs, costs go up'. By letting go of the sector budget's purse strings and trusting team sergeants to authorise overtime for their team members, the sector budget has never exceeded the limits set by the LPU. Whilst counter-intuitive, I believe this demonstrates the benefits of devolved responsibility. It also builds trust and is inherently more efficient than relying on the Sector Inspector to scrutinise and authorise every scrap of overtime incurred. As the sector budget is, therefore, permanently within budget, it means that, where appropriate, funds can be channeled into additional policing operations.

My policy towards 'managing' my budgets has always been the same. As a result, teams I led in different parts of the West Midlands Police force area have always remained within budget. This counter-intuitive approach has baffled many, who despite introducing strict budgetary controls and permission-based processes cannot understand why their own departments keep being overspent (it's because they do it that way). To respond to questions posed by those who look at my sector's figures and wonder why crime is relatively low, budgets are within limits and 'performance' appears 'good', the answer lies in this simple adage, which I have lived by since I was a young police constable: "If you do the right thing, the numbers look after themselves".

Summary

To summarise, things are brighter these days on the North East sector at Wolverhampton. The positive results achieved by implementing a systems approach were possible with the same resourcing levels, same people and same pressures as before. It just took a different mindset and a bit of trust.

The systemic changes implemented on the sector essentially happened in two phases:

- Stage One involved analysing the system, eliminating waste and refocusing priorities.

- Once stabilised, Stage Two involved reviewing and consolidating progress, improving the system and capitalising on freed-up capacity by introducing a new feature within the operating model (i.e. proactive function).

The common theme was removing waste to create capacity, which in turn created more capacity. Clear priorities and an unambiguous focus on quality resulted in a more effective system and an upwards spiral of continuous improvement. The experience also highlights the sub-optimisation and inefficiency caused by the waste activity and focus on performance targets that were commonplace until October 2010. The additional capacity created and ethos of organisational trust have proven to be powerful features of a new operating model that encourages innovation, as well as trust and devolved responsibility. We know we are doing *what works* to achieve *what matters*.

Where next? Well the results to date have been achieved despite the limited parameters I have been able to influence. A wider organisational shift towards systems principles and the introduction of measures against purpose would open the door to a more effective and responsive police service that extends beyond the boundaries of one sector on one LPU.

A (very short) Conclusion

I recently talked about what has happened on my sector at a high-profile national conference on policing. My presentation was titled *'Rocket Science: An Introduction'*. It was tongue-in-cheek, because it's not rocket science is it?

When I look back on it, the solutions were blindingly obvious:

Reverse everything that doesn't work. Take out the non-value activity. Replace it with *what works*, to achieve *what matters*.

That is all I did.

About the author

Simon Guilfoyle
Wolverhampton Local Policing Unit
West Midlands Police
Email: s.guilfoyle@west-midlands.pnn.police.uk
Twitter: www.twitter.com/inspguilfoyle
Wordpress: www.inspguilfoyle.wordpress.com

Simon Guilfoyle is a serving police inspector in the West Midlands Police, currently based at Wolverhampton. He joined the police in 1995 and has served as a front-line uniformed officer for almost all of his service. In 2011 he graduated with a Masters degree in Public Administration from the University of Birmingham. He writes and lectures on systems thinking and performance management, and his article on public sector performance management was published in *Policing - A Journal of Policy and Practice,* February 2012.

He uses his knowledge of systems and policing to maximise effectiveness within his workplace, and has provided assistance to other UK police forces that have requested advice on their own systems and operating models. He is also largely responsible for designing a victim-orientated process for dealing with lower-level crimes that has been widely adopted by police forces throughout the UK.

4. NO SOFT OPTION: CHANGING THINKING ACROSS AN ENTIRE POLICE FORCE

Chief Inspector Nick Bailey and Constable Steve Watson, Cheshire Police

This case study illustrates the following:

- Changing management thinking in an organisation dealing with issues ranging from murder to dog fouling is no soft option.

- Management by colours (red or green flags) is the soft option.

- Establishing measures that relate to purpose in a large organisation dealing with a wide range of issues takes time.

- It is easy to underestimate the true scale and influence of the target culture on decision-making at every level of the police, exacerbated by the Home Office, Her Majesty's Inspectorate of Constabulary and the Audit Commission.

- Some people think that measures are the same as targets and because they see targets as 'bad' they see measures as bad too. This view is hard to shift.

- Listening to customers is not the same as slotting what they say into categories.

- You can't copy thinking.

Background

Cheshire Constabulary is situated between the two metropolitan districts of Merseyside and Greater Manchester. It is a medium sized force policing a population of one million people within four unitary authorities – Halton, Cheshire East, Cheshire West and Chester and Warrington.

At the end of 2009 it had a workforce of approximately 2,200 police officers and 2,000 police staff. It was considered to be a low-cost police force with historically one of the lowest council tax precepts in the country.

The force has had a strong and successful culture of performance designed around a range of targets, set nationally, regionally and locally. It was rated second in the country for customer satisfaction and consistently performs well in relation to crime investigation when compared to national targets and peer review.

Cheshire Police has continued to innovate and lead the way in many modern methods of delivering a policing service.

Why the Vanguard Method?

The environment in late 2009 was one of uncertainty. The credit crunch and the banking crisis caused a sense of inevitability that government spending on public services, including policing, was likely to be cut. This was compounded by an impending general election and a perception that the government bodies that direct policing had not yet decided which direction to take.

Initial attempts at reviewing support departments to reduce costs were considered harsh, but these were nowhere near the savings that we would be expected to make: 10% of the total budget over three years.

The obvious option for many police forces was to review the organisation against threat, risk and harm. This methodology would grade areas of business where resources could be removed, dictating the future directions of cuts. 'Salami slicing' was a phrase only heard over the deli counter in Cheshire before this time, but the phrase became well known very quickly in policing.

Our senior management team and Police Authority had the foresight to recognise the limitations of such methods, particularly in terms of holding the service commitment to the public at the heart of the force.

Whilst some level of expertise for managing change existed in the organisation, it was accepted that additional support was necessary for the scale of the change. What was clear from the start however, was recognition that we would not be 'done to'. If we were to make real change we had to do it in a sustainable fashion to make sure it would withstand the uncertainty of the changing times. Ultimately, I don't think anyone anticipated the impact systems thinking would have on the organisation.

How we got started

On day one of the intervention, a Vanguard consultant said to the senior team:

"Do you know your demand?"

We replied:

"Of course we do, we have loads of crime data and call data. Sergeant, go and get the stats from the performance review team. Do you want them electronically, in paper, in colour? If there's one thing we know it is our data."

One hour later, after much discussion with the Vanguard Consultant, we said:

"Okay so we don't know all our demand, but we have still got all these stats .... what shall we do with them?"

In that hour we were given a lesson in really understanding our demand. We went to the call centre where all the calls from the public come in. We observed our great staff take a call, create an incident report and politely inform the caller what we were going to do.

We wondered what the point of all this was. Aren't consultants meant to tell you things?

But we had not done as we had been asked. We heard the call and saw a response but we had not listened. We accepted without challenge the call taker's interpretation and record of each call without correlating it with what the caller was really saying.

When we did listen properly, we heard within three minutes that we had turned a request for a crime number (for insurance purposes) into "I want you to investigate the theft of my mobile phone". Or we had turned a statement like "I've had a bump" into "I am reporting a non injury road traffic collision".

To return to our answer to the consultant's question...

"Okay so we don't know all our demand, but we have still got all these stats .... what shall we do with them?"

We learnt that Cheshire Constabulary had engineered itself to record and deal with the problems it wanted to handle. The system was designed to categorise and 'box' the calls for service as early as possible.

The purpose of this system is to give a pre-determined level of service based on the categorisation of the call which in turn is based on nationally recognised categories of crime and disorder. This method is subject to design, scrutiny, audit and assessment both internally and by national inspection regimes such as Her Majesty's Inspectorate of Constabulary. Whenever problems arise across the country, systems are reviewed to ensure that procedures capture newly devised criteria and that performance can be measured for compliance and comparison.

At this stage it was clear that our purpose, which our Policing Plan and literature say is to be focused on the public, was in reality focused on compliance and performance. Having decided to adopt systems thinking, where the focus is on the customer, it was clear we needed to change.

From this realisation came some clarity about principles and what we wanted to achieve.

Principles

- *Outside-in: What causes demand and what matters to communities?*
  Recognising that our purpose is to address the requests for service from, and the needs of, the public of Cheshire. Understanding that this includes the expectation that the police will keep the peace and protect the public.

- *Design against that demand*
  Seek to design service in line with the requests for service (made and unmade) from the public. Seek to stop doing those things that do not directly deliver a service.

- *Pay attention to flow: end-to-end*
  Understand the work that is required to solve the problem as
  it comes into the force, not as it comes into each department/
  unit/specialism.

- *Use measures to learn and improve*
  Have measures that show what works. Understand the
  relationship between measures to achieve and improve
  our service to the public and be purposeful.

- *Design for the predictable (common cause)*
  All services, from front-line to specialist, should understand
  (in terms of frequency, predictability, risk) and know their
  demand. Based on this, their design should be to service the
  80% that is predictable.

- *Contingencies for the unpredictable (special cause)*
  Contingency plans need to exist for the 20%. These are
  proportionate and may involve some level of risk management
  in the design of our organisation.

- *Person at first contact is the 'process designer'*
  The design of our service is based around the premise that,
  wherever possible, we resolve an issue at the first point of
  contact. Where this is not possible, handovers are limited
  and as much work is done as possible, with the best level
  of information possible at that time. There is a recognition
  that people on the front-line know what is required to
  deliver a good service. On this basis, they can state what our
  organisation should be able to provide and deliver – this is the
  process design. Where the design is 'top down' or specialised,
  this has the potential to compromise the service delivered to
  the public.

- *Managers line the system up behind the 'contact and decision'
  points*
  Managers seek to design the overall service to support the
  front-line service.

- *Don't specify the method. Use principles not procedures
  (unless very high risk)*
  The method is experimentation to solve problems. Policies and
  procedures can be restrictive. Guidance should be based on the

right way to work and understanding, by regular contact and observation, 'what good looks like'.

- *The managers' role is: clarity of purpose; help people develop and use data/measures; act on problems that get in the way of good work.*

Having identified these principles at a change team and strategic level, we were still some way from total organisational understanding. Policing is a 'can do' culture. This means we believe that good management is about making quick decisions and having solutions to problems. Crisis management is what we do. Therefore the expectation continues to be quick decisions, strong leadership and clear direction from the Chief Constable.

And clear direction is certainly what we got from our Chief Constable. He agreed a plan called 'Get Knowledge'. This would lead us to a new level of understanding about the demand and flow of work.

Check

The initial stages of 'Check' were about gaining a real understanding of the demand on the organisation.

In total we reviewed 22,000 demands for service on the organisation which included 14,000 telephone calls. This represented approximately two weeks' worth of demand. It took a team of fourteen staff four weeks to scope and review all the demands, recording them in a manner that reflected the caller's purpose and their actual request.

We included all routes where demand came into the organisation including calls into the call centre, visits to front counters and voicemails received in neighbourhood teams. Reassuringly for some in this age of technology, we also tracked demand that came by post and people approaching officers in the street.

It may have been an early scepticism or an innate need to have irrefutable evidence but, with hindsight, we did overwork the volumes to understand demand. However, this provided a credible base and an insight into the calls for service that Cheshire Constabulary receives daily.

In order to make sense of the data, 'High Level Demand Type' headings were agreed upon, reflecting the nature of the calls for service, represented in Table 1.

High Level Demand Type	% of Overall Demand
I want to report / give information	24%
Please turn up / stop something from happening	21%
Please give me some advice/ information	14%
Internal operational requests	13%
Can I have an update? / Responding to Police instruction	13%
External requests for support	12%
Abandoned / sales	3%
TOTAL	**100%**

Table 1. High Level Demand Types

From this representation, we identified that 'I want to report / give information', 'Please turn up / stop something from happening' and 'Please give me some advice/ information' were demand types that the public and police would accept as our purpose. It is what we are here to do.

The remaining categories however, represented calls that were either caused by our own internal processes or in the case of 'Can I have an update? / Responding to Police instruction' were the result of the police having done the wrong thing in the first place (failure demand).

The data showed us that 40% of demands on Cheshire Constabulary were potential waste. We could see that this was an opportunity for us to stop doing stuff which did not add direct value to our purpose from the public's perspective.

Breaking down the data further revealed that only 9% of calls we receive were recorded as a crime (in compliance with National Crime Recording Standards). This came as a shock to many in the organisation.

We isolated the top ten calls for service. The tables below show those which are recognised as either *value demand* or potential *preventable demand*.

Demand Type	Frequency (per month)
A traffic accident	1,674
About my lost property	1,186
A theft	1,116
Someone has / is trying to break in to my / a property	1,046
Nuisance youths causing problems / congregating in my area	942
I am / someone is being threatened	907
About suspicious people / activity	837
A missing person / not seen	837
I am being / have been assaulted	767
People throwing things at my property / vehicle	732

Table 2 - Value Demand

Demand Type	Frequency (per month)
Will you update an incident?	2,276
Can you put me through to a named Police Officer?	1,905
Will you record a crime?	1,633
Someone from outside the force wanting to check our systems	1,435
I want to speak to a Police Officer	817
I have brought my documents in	792
Someone from outside the force wanting to pass / share information	742
Will you put / update a critical marker on an address?	643

| Will you create an incident? | 594 |
| Can you do a check for me? | 569 |

Table 3 - Potentially Preventable Demand

For the first time this gave us a real insight into the demand placed on the organisation. Before we studied our demand, we would have said we received about 1,000 calls into the call centre a day. These were the calls we recorded when the public telephoned to report an incident and therefore these were the calls we captured.

What was not being captured however, were the additional 1,000 calls per day about matters we did not record. Because they weren't recorded, management had no idea what they were, who was dealing with them and how much work they were bringing in to the organisation.

This insight was, however, only the beginning of our understanding and learning. Different groups were despatched to discover more about the top ten demands and what was causing them. These later became pieces of work in their own right.

This is a flavour of what we discovered:

- 75% of the road traffic reports did not involve any injury to persons; under the legislation there is no requirement to report such matters to the police. On checking however, we discovered that insurance company advice to clients to not admit liability means that 'aggrieved' drivers want to ensure their claim will be accepted and want the police to witness the scene for future insurance claim disputes.

- We discovered that people report lost property to the police to get a reference number for insurance reporting, not because they have any real expectation of finding the property.

- When we assessed theft, we frequently asked the question 'why?' we did what we did. We learnt that the strong compliance regime and target culture constantly drives the decisions our staff make. We didn't find any understanding or systemic consideration of what action would prevent re-offending or the re-occurrence of the crime.

The influence of the target culture did not come as a great surprise to us, however the true scale and influence that such a culture has on every level of decision-making was unexpected. Targets influenced everything from the way we dealt with the initial call to the way we investigated crime and dealt with offenders. Such a culture had been caused and exacerbated by an inspection regime placed upon policing by the government through the Home Office, Her Majesty's Inspectorate of Constabulary and the Audit Commission.

The two pilot areas

We ran a number of experiments across the force area. One focused on the category of demand 'Missing Persons' and the other focused on one geographical area of Cheshire: Runcorn.

We chose to focus on the category of Missing Persons because it is an area of high demand that has a major impact on the individuals involved, some of whom are the most vulnerable people in society.

The purpose of the experiment in Runcorn was to learn enough (by applying the new principles) to start redesigning the whole force.

Pilot 1 - Missing Persons

We knew that Missing Persons was a top ten demand and possibly in the top three but we didn't initially have any reliable figures despite our recording methods. We estimated that the number of Missing Persons could have been between 3,000 and 5,000 for the 12 months before the pilot.

We settled on a figure of 3,800 for the purpose of the pilot. This was based on the quarterly returns the force sends to the Missing Persons Bureau. These returns are subject to manual checking before submission so we felt at the time that these figures were likely to give the best representation of the demand.

Understanding cost

To quantify the financial cost of missing persons to the police service is a complex task. The cost depends on the specific case although it's not unusual for an entire 'shift' or divisional 'block' to be involved in enquiries.

When front-line staff were asked, "What impact would it have on your day-to-day work if you never had another missing person report to deal with?", the answer was commonly "Well some days I wouldn't know what to do with my time". This was clear evidence that dealing with missing persons was taking a huge amount of time and resources.

For the purposes of the work undertaken in Cheshire, we used the figure of £1,000 per missing person incident. This is an average and does not take into account the true cost when including a multi-agency approach (which is often the case) which will be considerably higher.

The cost to the force when using the figure above was likely to be in the region of £3.8 million per year.

Understanding predictable demand

We wanted to find out if it would be possible to predict if a person was likely to go missing and then make sure the correct resources were allocated in advance. Or better, could we stop the person going missing in the first place?

To find out more, we examined the cases of people who had been reported missing eight times or more in the preceding 12 months. These persons were then known as the '8+ mispers'.

We found that in the preceding 12 months Cheshire Constabulary had dealt with 61 people who had been reported missing 8 times or more. These people represented 2.5% of people reported missing in that year. Between them they had been reported missing a total of 988 times, or 26% of the total number of missing person reports for the year.

In financial terms the demand created by these 61 individuals represented almost £1 million. Furthermore, most of these people had been reported more than 8 times, some on more than 30 occasions. This was certainly predictable behaviour.

At this point we knew that reports of Missing Persons represented a significant demand on the organisation and that by using a predictability model we could concentrate our efforts on a small number of individuals in order to make potentially significant savings. But who were the 61 individuals and where did they come from? Was there a common theme — in effect, a secondary area of predictability?

The first significant statistic was that all but one of the 8+ mispers was under 18, so this category was almost exclusively young people. The only adult was a mental health patient (and as our work continues there is evidence that this is a growing area of demand for missing persons). When we examined the remaining 8+ mispers we found that more than 80% of them were in care (care home or foster placement) at the time of the report being made.

We now had a clear direction for our attention.

Redesign

At the beginning of redesign we asked if our own system needed to be redesigned or, given that most of the demand was coming from young people in care, we needed to educate and challenge beyond our organisation.

The first problem we encountered was the lack of information flow between the care service and the police service. Perhaps the most well-known and high profile of these barriers is Ofsted which, through legislation, will not allow local authorities to give police forces basic details such as the name and location of all care homes in a force area (Paragraph 5, Regulation 7 of the Care Standards Act 2000).

So we did some old fashioned investigative work to map out the 54 care homes in the county using the Ofsted website. This in itself was quite an onerous task which would have been completed in a matter of minutes had those services involved in the problem been able to communicate freely.

Visiting care homes

We visited the 54 care homes on a 'fact find' and discovered some interesting data. Of the 54 care homes there are 42 'mainstream' homes and 12 homes for children with learning/physical disabilities. The 42 homes were the main focus of our attention as it was found that the level of care in the remaining 12 homes was of such a high level (with high security based on the specific needs of the children in their care) that they rarely reported any young person missing.

Of these 42 homes there were 7 local authority homes and 35 homes run by private sector independent providers. The 42 homes had a combined capacity of 125 placements/beds of which 25 were in the Local Authority homes, the other 100 in the private sector.

All placements in local authority homes were for local children; only 20% of placements in the private sector were local, leaving 80% of the placements from outside Cheshire.

Fact finding and building relationships

Once mapped out we visited all 54 care homes in order to complete two specific goals.

The first goal was to gain a full understanding of the care home system and to gather as much information as possible. We found out the full contact details, management structure, company profile (for the independent providers), individual bed capacity, copies of in-house protocols and operating standards for each of the homes.

The second goal was to use the opportunity to explain the reasons behind our visit, our purpose, aims and expectations of both our partners and those asking for our help.

We made it clear that we had evidence, albeit anecdotal at that time, that the police service was being used inappropriately as an extra resource by the care home establishment. We made it clear that if such behaviour continued, it could lead to sanctions including, as a last resort, reporting the establishment to Ofsted in order to instigate an inspection into its suitability and fitness for purpose.

These visits strengthened our assertion that there was a widespread abuse of police resources allied to inappropriate reporting standards.

We found out that young people were often reported missing from the care home because they refused to come in on time or because staff were not available to pick them up. Further comment revealed that there were many inadequate care plans which did not reduce or remove the possibilities of the young person going missing.

Results

At the start of the work, the top 5 repeat Missing Persons had all been reported missing more than 50 times each. Currently no one person has been reported missing more than 20 times and those that have been reported more than 5 times are under constant review. There is also evidence of enhanced partner working to deal with such issues.

The overall incidence of reports of young people missing from care has reduced by more than 75%.

There is also clear evidence of many upgraded care plans which have been pivotal in reducing missing incidents and therefore significantly reduced risks encountered by these young people.

We have also worked with more than 20 Local Authorities outside the Cheshire area to encourage them to revise care plans or move a young person to a placement that better suits their needs.

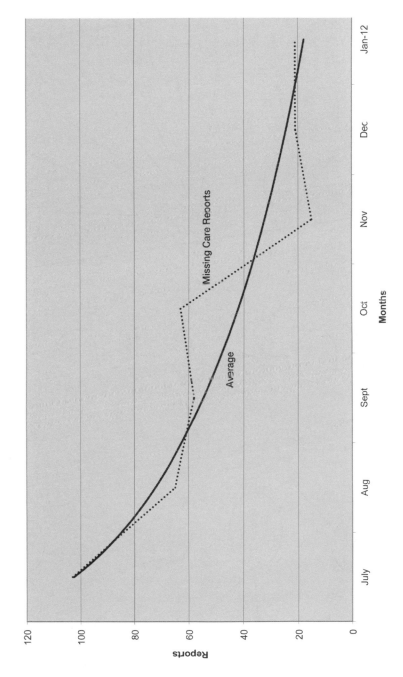

Northern BCU - Missing from Care reports

Historical abuse of the police service as a resource – a mind map

Partnership working

Initially, not all partner agencies welcomed our new approach. This is understandable given that higher-level care plans or more expensive placements may be needed in some cases. But this attitude has not deterred us because we know we are helping these organisations to reduce the risks to the young people in their care and therefore enhance the lives of those people and all concerned in their welfare.

Before redesign, we were good at finding missing persons and returning them to the specific care home but we were actually quite poor at challenging the care plans and care placements provided by those responsible for their care and well being.

Staff in care homes now feel empowered to challenge their area managers should they disagree with a pending placement (historically often based on finance) using our data as evidence to halt inappropriate placements.

Local children's services are now asking for our data so they can instigate their own changes and improvements ahead of police challenges.

Our own missing person coordinators, no longer overburdened with the demand fuelled by the care home system, can now allocate some of their time to associated issues such as young people who go missing from their family home or adults reported missing from hospitals or mental health institutions. This in turn will assist in reducing risk to other, high-risk groups.

We are now moving toward a care home system throughout Cheshire which undoubtedly provides a far better service to all its young people, who as a result are living in a safer environment.

Problems with codes

The internal reporting standards, incident opening and closure codes and associated control room quality assurance and data cleansing are an ongoing issue.

The actual size of the missing person issue also varies depending on the search parameters used. Although using the National Police Improvement Agency quarterly returns does address this to an extent, it's undoubtedly driven by poor practices at the initial stage in the control room.

An example of this would be an incident which is opened as a 'concern for safety' by the control room yet managed in its entirety as a missing person enquiry because this is what it later turns into. This is not a problem in itself as long as the incident is closed as a missing person incident (this is a searchable piece of data). However, the practice of closing incidents with the same code they were opened with has led to some serious underestimates in the number of missing person incidents. As this improves, incident numbers may be seen to go up despite significant reductions in actual calls.

This may well mean that the actual number of missing persons in Cheshire is closer to 5,000, costing the force £5 million, rather than the previously estimated £3.8 million.

However, this does not mean that the 8+ mispers were less significant or that 2.5% of the persons reported did not account for 26% of the demand. Quite the contrary, when we examined the 8+ mispers we found a significant number of incidents relating to these individuals were recorded as 'concern for safety' and not included in the original data set. Furthermore a number of individuals, when including inappropriate opening/closure code issues, would have been included in the 8+ misper figures.

We found that these data quality issues had almost no effect on the 'headline' figure of 2.5% of individuals accounting for 26% of the total of all missing person enquiries. Likewise, the demand from young people and the care system remained in excess of 80%.

Positive effects on young people

Although it may appear that many of the revised placements would simply be moving the problem to the care home, often outside the county of Cheshire, there was often evidence of the move having a very positive effect. For example:

Outreach Worker for a 15-yr-old in a care home:

> *"XXXX's life has been turned around following this move. Thanks to your efforts and 'persuasive' nature in challenging the previous placement we can now move forward in a very positive manner."*

Care home manager, referring to our intention to report care homes to Ofsted (to date we have never had to report any establishment in Cheshire):

> *"I'm in a far better position to influence the placements now I can remind my area manager of the work you are doing and the potential ramifications should we accept placements which are obviously inappropriate."*

Missing Person Coordinator, after reports of missing children in care reduced from 60+ per month to a recent monthly total of 9:

> *"For the first time since taking over this role I'm able to spend some time looking at the issues surrounding reports of missing adults. I've always been involved solely in issues surrounding children in care."*

Conclusions from the Missing Persons pilot

This case study shows that gaining a better understanding of demand allows for more informed decision-making. It demonstrates that children reported missing from a care home are not just a police problem and by working together to address the root cause and demand, namely protecting vulnerable children, this can be achieved systemically. By bringing together all those agencies involved and being clear about purpose, the number of vulnerable children reported missing has been reduced, the risk to children has been significantly reduced and considerable police resources have been saved.

Pilot 2 – Runcorn

The purpose of the experiment in Runcorn was to learn enough by applying the new principles to begin redesigning the whole force.

Before we started the pilot, we agreed four principles to guide our decision-making and that of our officers:

1. We do what matters to the victim (includes callers, customers, etc.)

2. We do what matters to the community

3. We act fairly/firmly with the offender (we want to reduce re-offending and future demand)

4. Whatever we do, we act in the public interest

The experiment began with one call from a member of the public, where we applied the principles, from call to conclusion. We sought to deliver the 'perfect' service and, where necessary, worked back from that.

In applying these principles we sought to do the right thing at the first point of contact with the customer and, if this was not possible, then to limit the handovers to those that were necessary to do what matters to the customer and the above principles.

In practice this meant diverting all non-emergency calls for Runcorn from our centralised call handling centre at headquarters to local call handlers at Runcorn. Each call was dealt with on the basis of the principles. From the start, call-takers were supported to provide a more comprehensive service and, where appropriate, deal with the call in its entirety or gather better quality information to help decide who to send out and when. Intelligence officers were deployed to sit with call-takers to help them understand the context of the call, any history and the most appropriate response.

When officers were deployed they were supported in applying the principles, even if this meant going against policy or procedure, just as long as the principles were applied.

Every call was reviewed end-to-end to learn more about the real cause of the call and to uncover issues which prevented the member of staff from doing a better job and to identify skills that would help them do a better job next time.

Early findings showed that staff were not available when many of the incidents occurred. By design, staff had adjusted to respond to a 'slow time' (non-urgent) model of response that suited the organisation, but had not been designed to give the best service to the public. In addition, the various 'specialist units' within Cheshire Constabulary had set clear parameters on when they would attend and support the handling of an incident. This meant that the first-line responders were unable to call in specialists when they were needed to meet demand.

We identified the following factors that prevented us delivering a perfect service:

- Number of handovers between departments
- Inability of staff to pull expertise from other units

- Inappropriate deployment of Police Community Support Officers (PCSOs)

- Inability to secure real time support for drug referrals

- Departmental targets

- Crime recording versus crime detection

- Deployment policy

- Silo mentality and associated ways of working

- Lack of awareness of problem-solving options

We learnt that the design of different departments with different targets caused varying levels of service to the public depending on, for example, the time of day when the incident occurred or the culture of the unit.

Observing and evidencing this meant that it was a simple decision to move from a dedicated response team who had no responsibility for dealing with community problems to creating a new team of staff who were able to respond to, and problem solve in, the community.

The decision to go against specialisms means that Cheshire is doing the opposite of what is being done in many other police areas. Delivery against purpose is counter to traditional thinking where delivery is designed against targets and perceived efficiency.

Results

- The number of 'slow time' tasks decreased significantly from 400 at any one time to a lowest of 60.

- The number of attendances at incidents (classed Grade 2 – i.e. quick response) increased and attendance times improved.

In practice, this means that officers are now able to deal with incidents as they are occurring, with better information and the freedom to do what matters to the caller instead of dealing with many enquiries in slow time (indirectly causing the organisation to have more operational staff on duty Monday to Friday nine to five, than at weekends and in the evenings).

Such behaviour was observed later when the principles were applied to wider areas.

Graph 1 demonstrates Grade 2 incidents which require a response at the earliest opportunity. The numbers rose immediately after the principles were applied in January 2011.

Graph 1

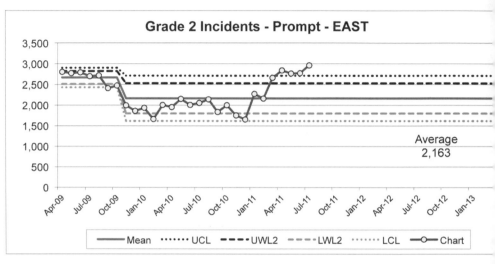

New measures across the entire organisation

We have no doubt that having the right measures is vital to demonstrate delivery against purpose. From the beginning of the pilot, questions most often asked by staff were "What are the new targets?" and "What are the new measures?" For a time we were searching for that undiscovered measure which, when found, would transform policing and give clarity for everyone.

The difficulty is getting some people in the organisation to realise that meaningful measures are not directed down, but come from those doing the work. Measures are necessary for continuous learning about what works to achieve purpose and those who are doing the work are best placed to measure what is important.

We ask the following questions of each team to help them to develop measures:

- What is demand and how do you understand what it is?
- What are you doing to reduce and tackle the demand?
- How do you know it is working?

Measures do, however, remain the hardest part of this change, highlighting the strong culture of targets that remains in the organisation. Our *de facto* purpose had become meeting the targets and this caused the organisation to work the way it did.

With the support of the Chief Constable, the organisation has begun to understand the requirement to make better decisions in line with purpose that will help reduce demand. However, the culture of policing is still very much about a quick 'solution' with little evidence base. As a consequence, some level of change in attitudes has taken place, but the use of data and measures to inform decision-making has been limited, with the view held by some people that because targets were bad, measures must also be bad.

As part of any other change programme, our limited success in developing good measures would be seen as a failure and the organisation would quietly return to a target and compliance regime. However there is a real understanding that our approach is the right thing to do and as a consequence the failure to use measures fully is recognised as part of the change of culture required and one of the system conditions that needs to be overcome.

The right measures will undoubtedly provide evidence of the success or failure of the changes we have made, but remain the hardest part to achieve. In the interim it is vital to have confidence that this is about doing the right thing and doing what matters. We have worked hard to outline our proposals to outside agencies that can help us achieve more, e.g. Her Majesty's Inspectorate of Constabulary, the Home Office and National Police Improvement Agency.

Staff

From the outset there was an initial scepticism from many staff that any change programme was a cost cutting exercise. The secondary issue was that in a traditional command and control organisation the 'Check' phase was initially viewed as 'being seen to do the right thing'. People thought that the Chief had already made his decisions.

It soon became clear, however, that the learning coming out of 'Check' was not the normal information. Over time, staff started to believe that the primary aim was to genuinely learn and provide a better service for the public, with reduced costs being a consequence of change and not the driver.

When we began the Runcorn Pilot, we learnt just how powerful the target culture was. Such was the belief that systems thinking was a passing fad that middle managers and front-line staff openly questioned senior managers and were reluctant to allow any changes to their processes for fear they would damage their performance figures, which would be held against them.

Whilst the austerity measures have undoubtedly had an effect on morale in the police and wider public sector, Cheshire Police staff now recognise that local decisions are being made with the best intentions for the public. As one officer told the Deputy Chief Constable "You know, boss, you're in real danger of improving the morale of the constabulary".

Below are comments from a staff forum held to assess the impact of the changes in Runcorn:

- "Big plus having everyone in one place."
- "Tasks are getting completed quicker."
- "We have more interaction with officers and PCSOs."
- "Don't think there are any disadvantages."
- "Closure of incidents is still an issue."
- "Personally I feel more motivated, it is more interesting and there is more interaction."
- "It's much better speaking face to face with officers and PCSOs."
- "The benefits are better with all staff in one place."

Leadership across the entire force

The change is driven directly by the Chief Constable and the Deputy Chief Constable, which in a command and control, hierarchical organisation is vital. This approach was adopted for the whole of the organisation from front-line policing to the specialist investigations. The attitude of senior managers to the changes has varied from full support and understanding to overt agreement with covert non-compliance.

What was seen in the early stages as the soft option by some (in that targets were removed) turned into a realisation that, for this to succeed across the organisation, it would take time and require leaders to change the way they managed. The drive for leaders to be 'in the work' and understand their role as enablers for the front-line takes time and is more intensive than management by colours – red or green.

In the early stages, leaders learnt how their directions and orders had been interpreted through the organisation and particularly on the front-line. For example, they learnt that a focus on levels of detected crime at a force level could be traced to an arbitrary arrest target in some teams.

Despite the system conditions, the Chief Constable remains focused on delivering the change across the organisation.

> *"Our officers have been, and continue to be, committed to keeping the people of Cheshire safe and creating an environment where they feel safe. A lot of the central direction and requirements are being taken away from us and we can now start to think about those people that really make a difference to the Cheshire public, what we should be concentrating on, and how we can work in different ways and concentrate on those things that really matter to the public.*
>
> *None of this is going to be easy. But I do know that it is going to make a big difference for our public."*

Dave Whatton, Chief Constable

> *"Fundamentally this is not about changing our structure, it's about changing the way we all think and how we challenge and think about everything we're doing in the interests of the public. It is never going to finish, it just becomes the way that we work, constantly thinking about the way that we are doing things.*
>
> *This is about looking at policing from a citizen's perspective and working out what is of value to them, and looking at what else we do and seeing whether that is a value activity and, if it isn't, then we stop doing it. This should mean that we can deal with more incidents with fewer officers.*
>
> *Early indications are that it is working — there are more officers available to attend incidents when we need them, and we are getting to more incidents than we were before."*

Graeme Gerrard, Deputy Chief Constable

Learning

During the re-design at Runcorn, leaders across the whole organisation were encouraged to visit and observe. They were also asked to view the boards outlining the data, root cause, learning and system conditions and blockers. The Runcorn experiment would set the foundation for changes across the whole of Cheshire Constabulary. Its success was in reassuring the senior leaders that the organisation needed to change and that the direction should be in line with systems thinking. Unfortunately the initial experiment was observed by many through traditional thinking, in that the changes made during the experiment were seen as structure changes, with a failure to fully understand the thinking or double-loop learning that needed to occur.

We have also reflected on the scale and the timescale of the change and whether this should have been carried out departmentally first as opposed to end-to-end across the entire organisation, even reaching in to partner organisations and processes (particularly the judicial and local authority processes).

Conclusion

There are many individual bespoke lessons for carrying out this change but the overarching lesson is that this has to become normal business and not a programme or project. We know that changing our thinking is the only way to improve an organisation the size of Cheshire Constabulary with such diverse demands, especially in the current economic climate.

Key to our success will be continued support by the leaders, particularly the Chief Constable and Police Authority, without which the scale of cultural change will be impossible to achieve. With this support the organisation needs to become one where learning and understanding are intrinsic to service delivery for the good of the public.

About the authors

PC Steve Watson
Tel: 01606 362011

Steve has twenty years service in Cheshire Constabulary, with much of his career being spent as an armed response officer covering the county. He says:

"A desire to test myself caused me to change direction and begin work in the force projects department reviewing the in-house work management system.

I have demonstrated a wider business sense as a successful designer of innovative products, and I bring this outlook to my duties within the police. As a consequence it was not long before I started to challenge the way the system works and I was quickly brought in to the force change team."

Whilst looking at several areas of demand on the organisation it has been my work on police response to reports of missing persons that has driven me to deliver systems which provide better outcomes for vulnerable children and reduce the work of the police and other partner organisations."

Chief Inspector Nick Bailey
Tel: 01606 363210

Nick has twenty-two years service within Cheshire Constabulary, spending much of his early career as a detective. He says:

I have since managed both detective and neighbourhood policing teams. I have predominantly worked in the north of Cheshire, in Warrington and Halton and have been responsible for delivering a number of joint agency initiatives supporting vulnerable people in the community, including 'Revolving Doors', giving me an initial understanding of what causes demand on the police.

Having been involved in the tail end of a previous force structure change in 2005, creating specialist departments, standard operating procedures and suites of targets, it was interesting to review some of my own designs through the work I have led for Cheshire Constabulary over the past two years."

5. STAFFORDSHIRE FIRE AND RESCUE

PUTTING OUT FIRES AND RESCUING PEOPLE

Becci Bryant, Director of Organisational Development

This case study illustrates the following:

- People 'in the work' are better at coming up with solutions than senior managers sitting in a darkened room.

- Anecdotal evidence is no substitute for getting knowledge.

- Rating performance as 'red' or 'green' prevents you from understanding what is really going on in your organisation.

- A system that allows people to cooperate towards a shared purpose (in this case putting out fires, rescuing people and preventing fires) is more effective than a system that encourages people to compete for resources.

- Understand what is going on in your system first and only then experiment with IT.

- Only collect data if it helps you achieve your purpose.

Context

Stoke on Trent and Staffordshire Fire and Rescue Authority serves a county of over a million people. The ageing population has considerable implications for the Fire Service because the people most likely to die in an accidental fire at home are over 65.

Stoke on Trent is ranked the 16th most deprived local authority area in the country. It is also in the top 10% of the most deprived areas in terms of income, employment, health/disability, education, skills and training.

Staffordshire Fire and Rescue Service (SFRS) has thirty-three fire stations with 1,163 personnel split between full-time, 'retained' (individuals who provide fire cover but it is not their full time occupation) and support staff.

In 2001 the service was re-structured and nine Area Commands were created, each with its own management structure and administration support. The geographical boundaries for the Area Commands were based on local authority areas. The principle behind this structure was to integrate our service delivery with partners and to make sure partnership work was at the heart of all our activities (Figure 1).

Figure 1: Map of Staffordshire Fire and Rescue Service

To support the nine Area Commands a number of centralised departments were established to provide a level of expertise thought not to be required at a local level.

Background

In April 2010 we set up a new Business Transformation Team consisting of Area Commanders and four other managers from the following departments: Performance and Planning, Strategic Risk, Administration and an operational Assistant Area Commander. Co-opted members joined the team when required.

As an organisation we had to make efficiency savings. We recognised that there was waste in our processes, duplication in our systems and a disconnect between some areas of the service. What we did not know was the extent of the waste because all we had was anecdotal evidence. Vanguard was invited in to support us and build up the skills within the team to create a self-sustaining approach. Toby Rubbra from Vanguard worked with us to develop a base level of skills and has continued to support us during our work.

The purpose of the new team was to review the organisation's structure and service delivery model. Within this work there were three clear caveats set by the Chief Fire Officer:

- No compromise to fire-fighter safety

- No compromise to community safety

- Protect as many livelihoods as reasonably possible

Between April and October 2010 the team carried out 'Check', focusing on the support received from various centralised functions.

Check

'Check' really stimulated us because we were challenging the fundamental thinking that led to our performance. In the first instance we needed to understand what our purpose was. This was from the point of view of the customer and not what we thought it was.

'Check' involved asking a number of questions and actually getting staff to show us the work rather than just talking about it. This in itself proved thought-provoking because 'following the work' created by demand is not something we would ordinarily do.

We asked a number of questions during 'Check':

- What is our purpose from the community's point of view?

- We have a legal purpose applied to us by the Fire and Rescue Services Act 2004. However, what is it we are *really* here to do?

- What are the demands that hit us, who are they from, how often do they hit us?

- What matters to our service users?

- How well do we respond to our demands and how effectively do we influence these demands? What is our capability to meet our purpose?

- What do we actually do to react to our demand and to pro-actively influence the levels of demand we receive?

- Do we know where our value or waste work is within our systems?

- Why are the systems we use like this?

- What is the thinking that has developed the current ways of working and, if there is waste or blockages, how can these be removed?

One of the crucial findings was the lack of easy-to-find data. We have over 60 systems used by different departments that do not communicate with each other. This led to duplication and triplication of effort when inputting data. It was vital that we had hard evidence to demonstrate the level of waste in the service so we could present it to our Strategic Management Board (SMB). We realised that we would need to prioritise which areas to tackle first in order to get approval from the Board to take action. We also realised that to re-design against these priorities, we would have to identify *de facto* purposes that were causing a loss of focus. Toby Rubbra helped in the development of the proposals but these were our findings and recommendations and not Vanguard's. This made the message far more powerful.

The four days

During August 2010 there was a four-day period which will remain unforgettable to those of us involved. It was during this period that we brought together hard data to provide evidence of the waste. The waste in some areas was so great that we had to count the data manually because we were not able to retrieve it from our systems. It was during the four days that we discovered how little we control some of our systems. We found out that we only crewed our fire appliances correctly for 17% of the time. This was staggering. It meant that for the other 83% of the time we either had more people than we needed or we were paying people to come in on overtime.

Rob Barber (Station Manager/Team Member) recalls those four days and says:

> *"The four days spent understanding both the demand entering the service as well as the number of training courses and other absences from duty had a significant impact. It was one of those moments that I realised how little we truly understood the organisation. The current systems did not inform us about the things that we need to know and understand in order to improve the organisation; rather they simply fulfil the requirements of some other external organisations or quangos. I feel that it was one of those times where the waters cleared and we realised what it was all about."*

What we learnt from Check

- We did not know the organisation as well as we thought we did.
- We had a series of *de facto* purposes.
- We collect lots and lots of data but never use it.
- We did not evaluate activities and initiatives and, therefore, we did not know how much they cost or whether they had the impact we were hoping for.
- Headquarters was creating a pull on the front-line deliverers rather than the other way around.
- We did not understand how much the system really cost.

Defining our purpose

Our *de facto* purposes were:

- Help partners achieve their outcomes.
- Perform against various indicator sets.
- Support the work of departments at headquarters.
- Fulfil the requirements of the National Framework for Fire and Rescue Service.

Our purpose is defined in the Fire and Rescue Services Act 2004 as a set of core duties including fire safety, fires and road traffic accidents, and emergencies.

So the question about our purpose from the customer's point of view still needed an answer. Although we thought we knew what it was going to be, Tony Rubbra encouraged us to ask our customers. Fire-fighters working in communities asked people the simple question "what is the purpose of the Fire Service from your point of view?"

The answer to the question was in the main, 'to put fires out'. However, some people thought it would be good if we tried to stop fires in the first place. From here we developed two purposes for SFRS:

1. Response – To put fires out and rescue people

2. Prevention and Protection – To do sensible things to prevent fires and other incidents occurring

Using the phrase 'sensible' in our purpose ensures mission creep is removed from our proactive work. The next crucial piece of work was to understand the relationship between the two distinct purposes and the only way to do this was by applying a new set of measures. Only then could we consider what the methods of service delivery would look like.

Re-defining our measures

For several years Best Value Performance Indicators (BVPIs), Key Performance Indicators (KPIs), and Local Area Agreement Indicators (LAAIs) have dominated our performance management system. We judged our success or failure on being either red or green. All our performance had been linked to targets that were set either nationally by government or locally by the Senior Management Team. Our indicators were numerically based and set against the previous year's performance. This way of thinking led to us focusing our attention on being green and not red. This meant that the understanding of how we were performing against our purpose was limited (creating a *de facto* purpose).

Hamstrung by targets

As Tim Hyde (Area Commander/Team Member) explains:

> *"One big issue we have had relates to a quote from Jim Collins 'Good is the enemy of Great'. I can relate to this as many colleagues, who refuse to see the benefits of statistical process control, have, for years, been told that we are an excellent service (having been*

examined by The Audit Commission) and all of their (poor) measures are perpetually green because that is what we chase."

We were so hamstrung by targets and BVPIs that we could not see beyond them. Following the demise of the centrally driven approach we took the opportunity to go through the pain of setting new measures without targets aligned to them."

Peter Dartford (Chief Fire Officer and Chief Executive) explains the rationale behind support for the removal of targets:

"It became increasingly obvious that the imposition of targets was failing to encourage our staff to do the right things. Their activities and our performance assessments became focused on the achievement of the targets rather than the delivery of quality services and the delivery of positive outcomes for the communities we serve. The move to use statistical process control as a performance measurement tool was introduced to reassert the need to focus on achieving community outcomes, rather than focusing on reporting the amount of work that had been completed. This will ensure staff have the freedom to do what they know are the right things in their locality, rather than what someone at the centre believes needs to happen."

A real understanding of performance

Before we moved to Statistical Process Control (SPC), Area Commands were consistently failing to meet targets more often than they were achieving them. There was no real explanation for this, and some debate about whether incorrectly set targets or poor performance was to blame. There has been a real reticence about letting go of targets and a fear that without them there would be nothing to drive improvements in performance.

But as Kath Bourne (Head of Performance and Planning) says:

"Having piloted the use of SPC we have not seen a decline in performance in the absence of fixed targets. Managers have stopped having repeated discussions about why performance operates at a certain level and searching for answers to 'what is wrong' for performance where the SPC charts clearly show that performance is operating within the expected norms. Focusing on the (relatively rare) occasions where performance breaks through the upper or lower control limits has given the organisation a trigger to know

where attention and resources need to be applied to performance anomalies. The use of SPC is helping us to distinguish between common and special cause and to moderate the way in which we manage the two issues."

Area commands and the dark arts

So now that we had a new purpose and a set of measures aligned to each of the purposes, it was crucial to try this new way of working within a geographical area of the service.

During 'Check' we visited all the Area Commands to find out what they thought of the way the organisation was structured. They said:

"We are not working together; it feels like the dark arts when trying to find out what is going on in other Area Commands." (East Staffordshire Area Command)

"The initial move to the nine Area Commands was the right thing to do so that the local communities' needs were understood. However, it seems that the competition between Area Commands in terms of performance and resources is now restricting the work that needs to be done, and the service focus seems to be missing. We should all be working towards the same goal." (Lichfield Area Command)

"The current Area Command structure allows for local interaction which is valued by staff and partners. However, due to the fact that the Area Commands cross cut a range of issues, they could be reduced in numbers." (Staffordshire Moorlands Area Command)

"The reduction of Area Commands would lead to clearer messages and information." (Cannock Area Command)

Re-design against new purpose

Following recommendations to Strategic Management Board, three of the previous Area Commands were joined together into one. A Lead Officer was then assigned to each of the new purposes along with a number of supporting managers. The resources from the Area Commands within the North of Staffordshire (Newcastle-under-Lyme, Staffordshire Moorlands and Stoke on Trent) were pooled together, and again aligned to purpose to form the new Northern Service Delivery Group (NSDG).

To support prevention and protection activities, a Community Safety Hub was established with direct links into the local authority areas to ensure there was no loss of service delivery to partners. This pooling of resources enabled us to target interventions on a larger scale, as demand required. Previously the Area Commands had their own resources but were unlikely to be supported by resources from another Area Command.

Testing the new approach

The first test of this approach came in December 2010 when we experienced an extremely severe house fire in Stoke on Trent that resulted in a fatality and serious injuries to one of the occupants. Immediately after this incident the prevention team were mobilised to the area to support the operational crews in helping the local community during an exceptionally difficult time. This was recognised as best practice at the time and the approach was maintained following other serious incidents within the NSDG.

Feedback from staff

To ensure the new approach was delivering from the point of view of the workforce, impact assessments were conducted and revealed the following:

"The prevention and protection hub at Quantum House has definitely made it easier to contact people, especially within fire safety. Our neighbourhood coordinator and risk reduction fire-fighter are excellent, and although the relationship with different staff has always been good, the current set-up and staff in post are the best I have experienced in terms of knowledge, the ability to assist quickly with issues raised through watch prevention work, and working together to serve the public in terms of both prevention and community fires safety."

"Our Watch Management team here on White Watch feel that having two distinctly different areas is helpful if speaking/emailing either Lead Officer is needed when discussions about specific issues takes place. Having one Station Manager dedicated to this station – overlapping both areas – is also helpful when required. Both informal (regular) and formal (less regular) face-to-face meetings are more effective with the same person answering any issues from middle manager level."

"I can see why we need a Lead Officer for each. I think it does help; each one can spend more time concentrated on one area."

Roll-in

In October 2010 the recommendations to SMB were supported and from January 1st, 2011 the new model was rolled-in. This is a continuous learning curve for those individuals now directly involved in this new way of working. The success of the approach has been that the work has been done *by* us *for* us, and not by a group of consultants that have parachuted into the service and then left. By using the Vanguard Method, we have developed a set of skills in-house that have taken us on the journey.

Helen Harrison (Group Manager/Team Member) explains her experience with the approach:

> *"Applying the Vanguard Method to Staffordshire Fire and Rescue Service has provided such sharp focus for us in relation to purpose that at times the noise of pennies dropping has been deafening."*

In summary, the advantages of the new model of 3 Area Commands each with a community safety hub are:

- A reduction in the number of senior managers and the associated savings.

- Alignment to purpose across a larger geographical area allows us to understand the impact we make in more depth because we are now looking at larger numbers.

- With a concentration across a larger area and a higher level of demand, Area Commanders have a greater appreciation of the impact their activities have and can ensure they are designed to absorb the type of demand hitting them.

- Splitting of the roles in line with purpose means the Lead Officer can focus on an area without the distraction of the other spheres of work.

- The hub draws together disparate resources that existed within the old structure so an area that may have had half a post allocated to it will now form part of a larger team approach. If anything serious happens then we can immediately put a bigger prevention team into that area without trying to borrow a resource from a neighbouring Area Command.

Fire safety at home

One of the key tasks carried out by all Fire and Rescue Services is the Home Fire Risk Check (HFRC) which involves a visit to someone's home to advise them on fire safety and to fit a smoke detector. Since 2001, we have been gathering information from occupants with the intention of using it to help improve the service in future. During 'Check' we reviewed the paper-based, 85-question form. The form was completed at an occupant's home and on return to station the form was passed on to the administration team who then input the data into the Community Fire Risk Management Information System (CFRMIS). As well as the waste experienced through the duplication of work there was a cost due to the use of paper and associated printing. Even more time was needed to check errors or blank sections on the forms with the person who submitted the form in the first place. During a three-year period between 2008 and 2010, the form we used changed, was adapted and grew. Between 2007 and 2010, 57,622 HFRCs were completed across the county.

A focus on data inputting

The time spent data inputting for these 57,622 HFRCs is shown in Figure 2. To understand this more fully, for the year April 2009   March 2010 it would have taken one full time employee 188 weeks of data-inputting to record the information from the 26,189 HFRCs that were completed. Importantly during 'Check', when we asked how much this information is ever used either locally or for returns to central government, we found out that there were only 10 questions that added value to the service.

Redesigning the form

It was clear that we needed to redesign the HFRC process.

To make sure the new way of working was the right way, we piloted a revised, more focused, form and the use of a mobile device for recording the information whilst with the occupier in their home. As the form was interactive, questions were linked to each other and the answers given would either remove further questions or highlight them for answering. The new form was piloted for three months before being rolled-in to the rest of the service in April 2011. Figure 3 shows the time (in minutes) spent inputting data from April 2011 to September 2011 in comparison to the time spent (in hours) during the same period in the previous year (and this was with a 10% increase in the number of HFRCs completed during the period in 2011). It is clear that the new method has reduced the administration burden considerably whilst at the same time providing data that fulfils our new purpose.

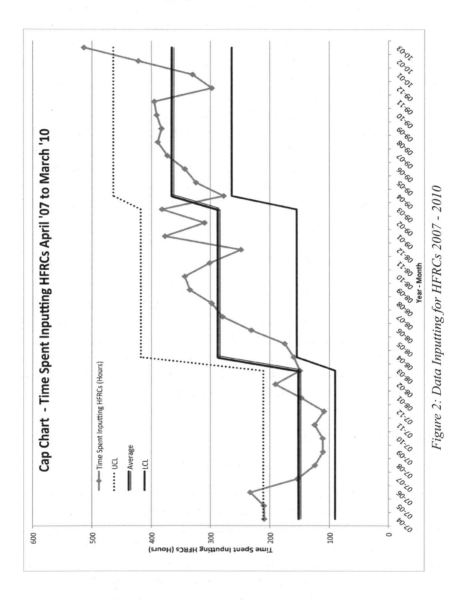

Figure 2: Data Inputting for HFRCs 2007 - 2010

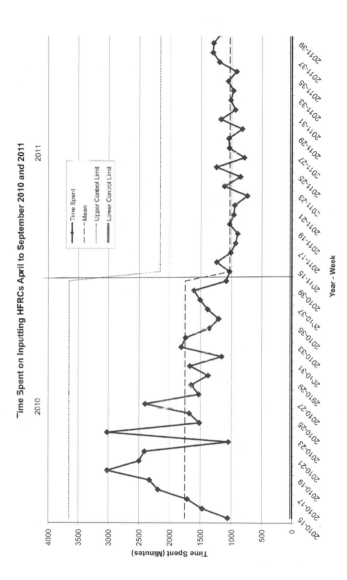

Figure 3: Data inputting with new way of working (April – Sept 2010 v April – Sept 2011)

Feedback on the new form

It was really important to get feedback from those who were directly affected by the new way of working so I sent out three simple questionnaires during the nine-month trial asking for feedback on both the new form and new mobile working. The following quotes come from people on watches, in the admin team, or in the prevention/protection team.

"The new form is much better as it appears to capture the obvious data that we would need. There are far fewer boxes to tick, etc., thus speeding up the time it takes to complete the paperwork when speaking to a customer, and allowing more quality time to discuss occupiers' concerns and individual circumstances, rather than appearing to read off a script."

"The new form is better, and with fewer questions that appear irrelevant to the customer, allows for a better delivery of HFRC. The reduction in codes to be used is also a time saver and should allow the forms to have a better accuracy level."

"The terminals have made the booking system more streamlined and efficient, and have obviously reduced paperwork/admin time on return to station as all work can be done whilst mobile. Once rolled out to allow stations to be completely terminal-based, this will be a big time saver for watch admin."

"There's a definite advantage in not having to print off paperwork for our appointments in the afternoon."

Helping vulnerable people

The data gathered from the new way of working is supporting the targeted approach to our interventions and allows us to understand in more detail the most vulnerable within the community. To ensure a holistic approach, we share information from the revised form with other public sector organisations when appropriate i.e. Smoking Cessation Services, Social Care and Health Services.

The benefit to the organisation has been that by trialling the new way of working in a small area we have been able to deal with the technical issues that have arisen; for example, we learnt which mobile device is the most suitable. Importantly we have not spent a considerable amount of money before determining that this method is the right thing to do.

Old thinking

We used to think that senior managers had all the answers. We thought, "We have always done it like this and it has worked so why should we change it or even want to change it?" We thought that because central government told us they wanted specific information, we must always collect it (even if it meant nothing to us and once sent to the centre we never got anything back from it).

A new culture

In an organisation of approximately 1,100 people, we now realise that all of those heads are better at coming up with solutions than just a small group locked away in a darkened room. We know we must focus more on our true purposes and the associated measures to really understand how we are doing. We now experiment with new ways of working and, if things do not get worse, then that is ok; but if they get better, that's great. It does not matter if you make a mistake or something does not work. Command and control is not the way to succeed in transforming an organisation.

Lessons learnt

- The intricate web that is an organisation is bigger that we realised.

- We were far more inefficient that we realised.

- Although our measures were showing green we did not really use the intelligence well to inform us (this is still an on-going learning process for us).

- Departments worked in isolation from each other without really considering the effect of their changes on the whole system.

- People must be empowered to contribute.

- We did not really understand the costs that different activities placed on the service.

- As a traditionally hierarchical organisation we thought we knew all the answers. The challenge to our thinking that Toby Rubbra provided was immense and painful at times.

Advice to others embarking on a similar journey

Senior team buy-in is crucial, along with empowering those working on the transformation to make decisions that count. If the people on the team are already credible within the organisation, then this adds weight to the approach. Involve the representative bodies from the very beginning if that is part of your working environment; they add great value and a different perspective.

The journey continues

We embarked on our journey of transformation some 18 months ago and it feels like we have only travelled a few hundred yards down the road. There is still a great deal of work to be done because the pilot and new ways of working were restricted to one geographical area. The restructure has released some additional capacity in order for the second phase of our transformation to continue.

The words of Wayne Bowcock (Lead Officer Response NDSG/Team Member) illustrate our commitment to continue:

> *"We are passionately committed to protecting the safety of our fire-fighters and the communities we serve but we know we can be more innovative to deliver our services differently whilst maintaining or enhancing these commitments."*

During this journey we have identified financial savings that equate to two-thirds of the £4 million savings that we need to make. This has all been done with no compromises to fire-fighter safety, community safety and the opportunity to redeploy personnel within the organisation thus removing the need for redundancies.

There is still a way to go to reach our predicted savings requirement of £4 million and so our journey continues.

About the author

Becci Bryant
Director of Organisational Development
Staffordshire Fire and Rescue Service
Tel: 01785 898542
Mob: 07971893240
Email: r.bryant@staffordshirefire.gov.uk

Becci Bryant is the Director of Organisational Development at Staffordshire Fire and Rescue Service. She has held this post since September 2011, before which she held a number of roles within Area Commands. She has also served at Cheshire Fire and Rescue Service and Bedfordshire Fire and Rescue Service, which she joined as a fire-fighter back in 1992. Most recently, whilst undertaking the Executive Leadership Programme, Becci gained a Certificate of Strategic Leadership and was the only person in her year to receive a commendation for her work during the course.

As well as providing strategic leadership, the main part of Becci's role is to drive the transformation process and ensure the delivery of the changes necessary to meet the financial challenges that will be faced over the next four years. This involves the implementation of redesign across the service, something that she has been heavily involved in since its initial development in 2010. Becci also has responsibility for developing collaborative arrangements with partners, and has managerial responsibility for planning, performance and operational assurance. Becci is also involved in the LGBT Network and Steering Group within the service.

6. 'DESIGN TO UNDERSTAND' IN HEALTH AND SOCIAL CARE

NHS SOMERSET AND SOMERSET COUNTY COUNCIL

Ann Anderson, Deputy Director, Strategic Development, NHS Somerset

Fred Parkyn, Service Re-Design Manager, Adult Social Care, Somerset County Council

This case study illustrates the following:

- Building relationships and understanding what 'a good life' is from the perspective of the individual, rather than 'pushing' standard services, products, processes and commodities, is key to helping individuals solve their real problems.

- The more we standardise and functionalise services the less we understand what matters to people and the less able we are to help them.

- The counter-intuitive act of putting more resources and expertise at the beginning of the process delivers better outcomes and savings over time.

- People-shaped solutions are often simpler, more effective and cost less than service-shaped solutions.

Background

This chapter is about transforming health and social care in Somerset to 'reable' people to maintain their independence and do the things that matter to them.

The term 'reablement' has a variety of meanings referring to a wide range of services, interventions and treatment goals. However, the main purpose of reablement is:

- To enable patients or their carers to be experts in their own care and avoid care solutions which foster dependence

- To support people to stay in their own homes for as long as possible and prevent inappropriate admissions to hospital and long-term care

- To ensure people are able to access effective and holistic reablement in a timely way and remain independent for longer in the community, reducing inappropriate admissions to hospital and care home placements

- To focus on supporting people to regain life skills and control, enabling them or their carers to be experts in their own care and avoid behaviours and care solutions which foster dependence.

Reablement in Somerset has developed over many years and is provided in a range of settings and by a variety of providers. This has led to a lack of clarity in roles and relationships between services. Overlaps and gaps have been identified.

Reablement was identified as a key priority for both NHS Somerset and Somerset County Council within the 'Delivering Independence' and 'Quality, Innovation, Partnership and Prevention' (QIPP) Programmes. Both organisations have recognised the potential for significant gains in terms of service quality, patient (the term patient is used to represent both patients and service users) outcomes and productivity and for increased partnership working with both private sector and voluntary and community sector organisations.

This joint priority provided an exciting opportunity to explore ways of improving outcomes for people with reablement needs, achieving a more integrated, whole-system approach, and using resources more effectively.

A key challenge for this project has been the defining of the scope and boundaries of the work within the existing complex rehabilitation provider landscape across Health and Social Care.

Why we had to change

When people think of health and health care, it is often hospitals that spring to mind. However, the great majority of people do not need hospital care in any given year. Over 90% of all contact with the NHS takes place outside hospital, in people's homes and in other community settings.

Effective and efficient community rehabilitation services aim to support people to stay healthy and ensure people can live as independently as possible and for as long as possible within their own homes, and to have the best possible outcomes in terms of quality of life.

However, primary and community care must evolve to meet changing circumstances. Advances in treatment are allowing more care to be provided in local communities, people in Somerset are living longer and we are facing greater public health challenges from obesity and other 'lifestyle diseases'.

Historical approaches to reablement are scattered across the NHS and social care organisations where all staff work hard in their functional islands. They 'assess' patients, 'treat' them and if necessary refer them on to other appropriate services, often not knowing whether other interventions are successful.

Many of these people continue to present at GP surgeries, A&E, outpatients and social care services despite numerous interventions by health and social care staff; each intervention has its associated costs in time and money.

The Vanguard Method was chosen to support the change to a more localised, integrated approach to reablement.

Check

We started by studying our system. We undertook a range of 'Check' activities to understand current demand and to find out what was really going on. This ranged from mapping current services across health and social care, understanding where and when demand entered the system, what people were asking for and what mattered to them.

Professionals from across the health and social care system collaborated enthusiastically in building up an understanding of how each part of their respective system currently worked, identifying many overlaps, gaps, duplication and frustration.

Throughout this process we validated what we were learning with a wider group of stakeholders.

Detailed analysis of patient journeys through the system proved particularly helpful in understanding what was happening over time, how the system was intervening in their lives and their experiences and outcomes. Five patients were followed in the detailed analysis over a two-year period. Over this time, there were a total of 71 GP contacts, and 20 hospital admissions of which 70% were for non-medical reasons. These five patients used a total of 415 bed days over this period and, despite the fact that all of them wanted to remain in their own homes, the outcomes were as follows:

- Three of these patients are currently in residential care

- One patient has 24/7 care at home

- One patient has died

New thinking

The new thinking involved first looking at how the parts of a service come together to produce the whole that the patient experiences. Often taking such a perspective reveals a significant opportunity for improvement, as conventional management thinking encourages us to concentrate on improving the parts rather than the whole. The new approach requires a real understanding of why are we doing something, before considering how we do it more effectively.

Once the new perspective has been taken, the second stage is the intervention theory – how to make a change. This approach highlights that there are two orders of change:

- **First order:** doing more or less of the same sort of thing (i.e. doing the wrong thing righter)

- **Second Order:** doing a different sort of thing. This requires us to stand back, reframe and challenge the (often implicit) assumptions and operating principles of the current system.

A new purpose

Our complex health and social care rehabilitation and reablement systems have grown over many years and are largely driven by political policies and targets. There was a real danger that the functional targets and objectives had become the *de facto* purpose. One of the key objectives of the Rehabilitation/Reablement Programme is to ensure that the real purpose, the patient's purpose, is clearly articulated and becomes the driver for recommendations regarding future service models.

The following common purpose was agreed for the new service and takes into account the feedback received from the patient consultation:

> *"I want to maintain my independence: help me to find the solutions to do the things that matter to me. The things that matter to me are:*

- *that you listen to me*

- *that you understand me and my needs*

- *that I do not have to repeat myself*

- *that you respond in a timely manner*

- *that it is easy for me to access the services I need*

- *that I am in control*

- *that you do not pass me from pillar to post*

- *that you respect me"*

Redesign

We decided to test a new reablement model, based on the principles above, investing more time and money up-front when responding to referrals for reablement. This emerging model tested the hypothesis that investing resources and time at the beginning, to understand the real problem that needs to be solved, saves time and money later.

A new team, called the 'Integrated Support Service' (ISS) team was set up. This involved:

- One GP surgery, including the District Nurse, Pharmacist and Community Matron.

- A single telephone number for referrals.

- An ISS team with five team members (Health Occupational Therapist, Health Physiotherapist, Adult Social Care Occupational Therapist, Social Worker, Care Worker Supervisor).

- One key worker per patient.
- Simple paperwork and minimum criteria.

This ISS team was given 'permission' to test different ways of working, and was not constrained by organisational barriers and systems. Wherever possible, the team did the work, ensuring a minimum of hand-offs and establishing good direct relationships and communication with the GP practice.

The old model

Old practice involved health and social care practitioners assessing, treating and, in most instances, referring people on to other services.

We know from the evidence that this method is far from effective in maintaining independence. It often results in costly and ineffective solutions and further admissions to hospital and long-term care, mainly because the underlying problems are not fully understood.

The new reablement model

The model that the ISS team now uses is based on the new purpose and principles.

The new service mantra is 'light touch, right touch' and its aim is to help people solve their own problems, maintain them in their own context, and to manage their own lives. New practice therefore involves understanding people in the context of their lives and what matters to them, helping them to re-balance by working out the right person-shaped solution to tackle the real problem and then setting them back on track to move forward confidently with their own life.

The test phase ran for five months. Qualitative and quantative data showed that there were encouraging signs of successful outcomes. This needed to be tested on a larger scale so, over the next six months, a further 15 GP surgeries in Taunton Deane were 'rolled-in' to the new way of working. This resulted in the creation of a further five ISS Teams.

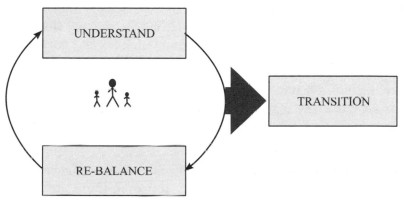

• Problem not always problem
• Understand whole situation
• Time to listen to learn "why"
• Trust

• Right touch, light touch
• Flexibility around traditional roles
• Identifying what is modifiable
• Easy access to GP, pharmacist, etc.
• Key worker is key provider

New service criteria

The new service criteria are minimal. Specifically, we do not apply the Fair Access to Care (FACS)[4] criteria. To qualify for a service, users simply have to be over 18 and registered with a Taunton Federation GP. The intention is to develop and provide a service that fits the needs of the population: historical working practices show that the development of eligibility criteria leads to individuals falling between services, and their needs often then escalate into a crisis.

The old eligibility criteria were designed to meet the service's needs not the individual's needs. There were early concerns and anxieties about the potential for new demand to emerge from fewer criteria. However, the delivery of the service within the resources has, for the most part, been achieved.

Where it has become clear that some cases are not wholly suitable for the ISS, these are managed on a case-by-case basis by the team deciding, through discussion, on the appropriate agency for their needs to be met.

---

4 http://bit.ly/HbtO0C

A new referral process

The new referral process is by telephone conversation direct with a team member. Each team arranges to make a registered staff member available on a daily basis to receive referrals by telephone from the GPs and surgery staff, the Acute Hospital wards, and Community Hospitals, as well as traditional referrals forwarded from Adult Social Care and the Adult Rehabilitation Service.

We have identified that referral forms and templates are not as effective in the transfer of knowledge and information about an individual as a real conversation. The referrer is encouraged to have a conversation with the team about concerns and gauge urgency.

The teams aim to see all referrals within the timescale recommended by the referrer, commonly two to three days. However, teams are able to prioritise urgent cases in order to prevent a crisis and aim to be available within one hour if required.

Two members of the team undertake the first visit to the individual and spend time listening to the patient and their family, understanding the problem and identifying what matters to them. This process is based on each team making use of the diversity of skills within the team, enabling a more effective understanding of needs, problems and innovative solutions. Regular interdisciplinary team discussions are essential to ensure that the skills and experience of the whole team are incorporated in the development and evaluation of the individual's support plan.

New documentation

Each team now completes a single shared document called 'Understanding You', replacing the single assessments from each profession. This builds a clear picture of not only what the person is able to do or has problems with, but also who they are, what is important to them, how they choose to live, and what their 'good life' looks like. This document forms the basis of the support plan that is left in the person's home, and will be updated as more is understood about the person and their goals and barriers.

The support plan is agreed with the individual and the team with the intention of attaining the goals over a six- to eight-week period. The support plan identifies the individual's specific goals, how they will be achieved and what the individual is responsible for doing. It also has the contact details for their key worker and team details. If expertise is required that the team doesn't have, this expertise is pulled into the team and incorporated into the support plan rather than triggering a referral to another service and returning to the former system of separate islands of help.

The role of the key worker

Each individual accessing the service now has a key worker from the team. This is usually the team member who has the majority of the contacts in delivering the support plan and has a strong and effective relationship with the individual. The key worker is responsible for coordinating the elements of the support plan and is accountable for the individual and their plan. The key worker is the main point of contact for that individual.

The role of the domiciliary care workers

Three preferred provider care agencies in Taunton provide staffing for two of the teams and these paid care workers are important members of the teams, enabling care support to be accessed immediately and flexibly. Being an integral part of the team gives care workers an additional awareness and understanding of patients' changing needs, whereas previously care workers were isolated from decision-making and planning.

A new approach to hospital discharges

The teams now have closer involvement in hospital discharges. The referral consists of a conversation with the ward-based staff about the barriers and problems experienced by the individual, and a discussion about the possible ways of supporting the person to be at home. It has taken time to engender a trust relationship in the service as the new model is able to provide services in a different way to that traditionally deployed.

The teams encourage positive risk-taking to facilitate discharges as soon as is practical, with rapid review at home and a capacity to amend plans quickly as required. It is acknowledged that people often function differently once in their home context, and so the understanding process is usually most effective if it is started once people have gone home, to prevent duplication and false assessments.

The transition from being supported to self-management

As part of the support plan, the team identifies what support systems will be required by the individual to enable them to self-manage their needs in the longer term. Work towards this transition phase is integrated into the reablement process. Some individuals may require extensive intervention to develop their self-management techniques and these would be considered as part of their reablement goals.

The teams have developed a model of intervention based on personalisation and professional reasoning. If the team identifies a task that will require ongoing input from another agency or worker, the key worker will draw that new worker into the team and undertake a careful transition of responsibility to the new worker, ensuring all the understanding of the patient is not lost at a handover point.

A new approach to communication

All communication to key staff, such as the individual's GP, follows the principles of reducing processes that do not add value. Conversations by phone are encouraged as are short, secure emails to transfer information. This enables the key information, specific to that individual, to be transferred efficiently and effectively rather than providing additional information through letters, forms or templates.

The relationship with the GP practice is maintained though providing the GP with a short summary of work by email or phone at the end of intervention.

A new management structure

Early implementation of the team's day-to-day support is provided by project leads to support the new model and operating principles so they become embedded into everyday practice. As teams developed in number, a new role was required to support the teams operationally with day-to-day management tasks.

A preferred management structure was developed with the intention of testing this in the Taunton Deane area and supporting inter-organisational working. Two managers, one from Adult Social Care and one from Somerset Partnership NHS Foundation Trust, job-share the management of the six teams, each taking lead responsibility for three teams.

A Partnership Agreement was developed to provide a governance structure to support this working arrangement, which details the lines of responsibility and accountability for managers, teams and organisations.

A new approach to administrative support

The intention is that, rather than making assumptions based on previous practice about what is needed, the administrative systems will evolve in response to demand, and be designed against actual need.

Capacity versus demand

The planned resource for each team was based on the level of referrals from practice populations previously received by Adult Social Care and Community Rehabilitation Teams.

Each team, as it has taken on its full population cohort, has experienced a period of more demand than it can cope with. Traditionally, services introduce tighter criteria or have waiting lists to manage such demand. However, this does not enable the service to meet its purpose, and during this test period some additional resource has been added to teams to meet this demand.

We have learnt from the experience of the earlier teams that, although there is a surge in additional workload in the first months, the referral rate eventually stabilises as those individuals with complex conditions have become known and understood by the team, and future contacts with these individuals are reduced. Our experience is that a balance between demand and capacity can be achieved without recourse to traditional demand management approaches such as eligibility criteria or waiting lists.

Flexible working across teams in times of high demand has been encouraged. Fundamental to the way the teams work is the concept of sharing skills and looking across the team to see what skills are most appropriate in any given situation and not being confined to traditional roles.

Culture

Bringing together staff from three organisations has been challenging, in part due to the differences in culture that exist between the organisations. This can be seen at many levels and it is important that teams identify common ground and work in a joined-up way to complete an 'Understanding You' with each individual.

Health care staff are naturally preoccupied with the human body and the functional consequences of ill health. Social care staff are focused on the functional skills and the impact of the environment, family and community that support them.

It has taken time for staff to appreciate the value of each other's different skills and areas of expertise and to develop strategies for incorporating all of these skills in the care-planning for an individual.

The most challenging change in culture and practice is encouraging the teams to be self-managing and return to professional reasoning and personalised care-planning. As services have evolved it appears that an over-dependency on processes has developed, together with a need to get authorisation to deliver services. Over time, this culture has created a dependency in the staff on process. It has also affected the ability of some staff to use reasoning and consider the best or most appropriate opportunities for the individual.

Across the staff groups it has taken time to adjust to the team holding a caseload rather than individuals holding a caseload which means sharing the responsibility for the support plan and interventions.

Information sharing

It has been essential to develop a collective vision for information-sharing and governance across the partner organisations. Early barriers to effective working were based on not having easy access to computers for processing data in the existing organisations' IT systems, not having a single record for interventions by team members, and double entering of information across organisations. This was further complicated by no one unique identifying number being readily accessible for the individuals; health care staff used NHS numbers and social care staff used a different number generated by their IT system.

Challenges for Adult social care managers

Adult social care has traditionally worked very closely with health services in Somerset. However the challenge for managers was that the integrated model raised many more cultural issues than we would have expected and the blurring of organisational boundaries proved challenging for staff and managers alike. We recognised there was a difference between working in a multidisciplinary way (old world) and following a new interdisciplinary model.

Although social care staff have liked the new model, described by some as 'old fashioned social work', they have been frustrated at the speed with which the organisations have been able to reduce the constraints that block working in this new way.

Social care staff are also now able to do preventative work whereas previously the 'Fair Access to Care' criteria meant they were only working with people who had critical and substantial needs.

Over the years, adult social care in Somerset, like many other local authorities, has introduced processes and policies that are designed to reduce spending and in doing so, has disempowered workers and undermined their ability to rely on their professional judgement. Working to this new model has liberated workers to become more creative and to do what they want to do, which is understand the problem and achieve success by using their skills and knowledge. However, some workers have found this new model difficult because it takes them out of their comfort zone. As managers, we have had to support workers to embrace change.

The impact on adult social care services outside ISS has been significant and it has meant we have had to review all the systems and processes with which we have worked for years. This project has not been an isolated piece of work – its tentacles have reached to the furthest corners of Adult social care.

Challenges for health managers

Health services have, in most cases, been developed by provider organisations, adapted and added to over many years to meet changing demand and top-down standards and targets. For health commissioners, when working with provider organisations to redesign services, the complexities of the systems already in place often present a considerable challenge to the goal of achieving better outcomes for patients. However it is clear from our stakeholder feedback that health staff working within these complex systems are aware of the constraints these systems put on their ability to do their jobs well.

The most important element of the initial work on this programme was identifying the 'purpose' of reablement services, and doing this from the patient's perspective. This was harder to do than anticipated because the language used in health care frames services from the perspective of the service provider. However, once achieved, this seemed very simple and straightforward, and enabled us to design against the real demand rather than perceived demand. Health staff within the teams have welcomed the new way of working and the opportunity to spend more time understanding the patient and, therefore, more effectively supporting patients to achieve what matters to them. However health staff are equally frustrated that it takes longer than they would like to deal with the organisational constraints that have emerged and which are so ingrained within our current systems.

Delivery of safe and high quality services is critical to all health service commissioners and providers and there are a number of mechanisms and frameworks in place across organisations to provide assurance in these areas. The key challenge for health managers when supporting the reablement pilot was to ensure an adequate clinical governance framework was in place, whilst retaining the flexibility to learn and to adapt the model throughout the development phase. This continues to be an area of learning and has required the strong support of provider organisations.

The other key challenge for both health commissioners and providers is to understand the impact of this service redesign on other areas of health service provision, and to gain a clearer view of how this programme links with other initiatives being delivered across acute and community settings.

New thinking about cost

In service organisations, the majority of cost is in the time of professionals. The plausible logic is that if we can control that amount of time then we will save money.

This manifests itself in the system in a focus on productivity and the length of transactions, for example, 8-minute GP appointments in the surgery, 12-minute average handling time targets over the phone at the call centre, kitchen assessments in the hospital kitchen rather than in patients' homes.

The consequence for performance is that the patient has to repeat himself or herself, feels passed around and will often re-present repeatedly in the system because their real problem still hasn't been understood or solved.

Alternative Principle – Design to Understand

For those patients with non-straightforward issues, this might mean taking more time and going to their own environment. When this is done we learn that the presenting problem is quite often not the actual problem. Front-line workers can then build solutions to address the cause of the problem, rather than transact with the symptoms.

The effect on performance is that the patient receives help for their actual problem, decline in the patient's condition is avoided and the system saves on expensive support.

The problem with functional design

The logic behind functional design is that, if everyone is given a smaller part of the process, then they will become very good at doing that bit and the overall speed and quality will improve. However, this flawed logic leads to functional islands of help with many hand-offs, over-specification, duplication and re-work.

The consequence for the patient is frustration and for staff it can mean being denied seeing the end result of their labours, and extra cost for the organisation.

Alternative Principle – Retain Ownership and Pull Support

A key worker is selected who will have responsibility for that patient and will pull support if the problem is not one they can solve on their own, rather than referring on to another professional to begin the process of understanding afresh.

The patient establishes a relationship and trust, and the system can design a patient-shaped solution which can change in line with the patient's needs. Staff get to know the people they are helping and can see their progress. Although the professional might spend more time with the patient, the system spends less time and money overall.

The following examples show what would have happened to patients in the 'old world' and what happens now.

Example 1 - Prevention of admission

Mrs L was referred by her GP as being frail, and suffering from sickness and diarrhoea; she was not eating or drinking. The GP reported that he would have usually admitted Mrs L to hospital if the team were not able to support her at home. In the new model, two team members visited Mrs L within an hour of the referral, and identified that Mrs L needed some support whist she was unwell. Mrs L was reluctant to have help at home, but also did not want to be admitted to hospital. The care worker was one of the team members who saw Mrs L at home, and was able to reassure her that it would be herself that would be visiting later that day to help her prepare a meal.

This continuity and familiarity with the same two members of the team carrying out many of the visits enabled Mrs L to feel confident about having a support package at home. The care worker spent time during the care visits developing a relationship and understanding of new worries and anxieties, and this enabled Mrs L to feel confident when other team members visited her.

Developing this relationship enabled the team members to identify a number of symptoms that were of concern, leading to the GP being drawn in to diagnose further medical problems. Once trust and a relationship had been developed, she was open to making other changes in her life; she had been using her husband's walking stick, which was the wrong height for her, and she benefitted from some general exercises to improve her mobility. She was also given some small items of equipment to support her safety at home.

By gentle encouragement and understanding the care worker enabled Mrs L to start to eat small meals then start to prepare snacks and drinks again. As a result her health started to stabilise and she gained strength and confidence. After two weeks she was able to continue preparing and eating drinks and meals, supported by her family for shopping.

Example 2 - Hospital Discharge

Mrs G has mild learning disabilities and hydrocephalus. She was admitted to hospital with vomiting and diarrhoea and the hospital team initially felt that she would require a nursing home placement. She was referred to the ISS team with incontinence and needing help from two people for transfers.

She wanted to return home and had been managing at home with some support prior to her admission. Therefore, in the new model, it was agreed with the hospital team that she should go home with an intensive package of support and be given the opportunity to see if returning to her previous situation was possible. She received a package of care with two carers visiting twice a day plus night care to understand and manage her night-time incontinence.

Mrs G identified what was important to her, and the Occupational Therapist developed a consistent regime with her so that she could learn to do her own breakfast for the first time. The physiotherapist had been practising transfers with the care worker and her care visits were reduced to one carer and appropriate equipment. Her key worker worked with the District Nurses to share the information and understanding about her night-time needs, so that a suitable management plan for her continence could be developed. The District Nurse reviewed and modified this plan and the night support could then be removed. Mrs G improved in all her abilities and has remained at home.

Learning

Our key learning can be summarised as follows:

- Minimal criteria will lead to more efficient use of resources in rebalancing the individual at an earlier stage, and so deliver better outcomes and savings over time.

- Eligibility criteria and waiting lists lead to people falling between services, their needs often ignored and their situation later escalating into a crisis.

- When removing eligibility criteria, there is an initial increase in workload. This stabilises when people with complex needs are understood and further contacts with the same person reduced.

- Not understanding underlying problems in a health and social care setting can result in costly and ineffective solutions and preventable admissions to hospital and long-term care.

- The presenting problem in a health and social care setting might not actually be the real problem. Taking time to understand people in their own home and context allows workers to build solutions to the real problem instead of providing transactions to deal with the symptoms.

- Real conversations between professionals about patients are more effective than referral forms and templates, especially when trying to judge the urgency of a situation.

- Administrative support should evolve in response to an understanding of demand and not be provided on the basis of previous practice.

- The consequence of a functional design for the patient is the feeling that they are being 'passed from pillar to post'.

- When people from different organisations come together to agree a single common purpose from the point of view of the patient, working together becomes more straightforward and productive.

- The allocation of resources should not be based on historical configurations and complex systems. Resources should be configured around the needs of the patient.

- Front-line staff are usually well aware of and frustrated by the system conditions that are preventing them from doing their job.

- Giving individuals a key worker who has responsibility for either solving the problem or pulling help if the problem is not one they can solve on their own, avoids the cost and frustration of multiple assessments.

Results

The qualitative evaluation of the pilot has shown very positive results from patients, staff and clinicians. The responsiveness of the service and the focus on individual need is very much welcomed and is considered to have resulted in an improved quality of service provided to individuals and an overall increase in staff motivation and satisfaction.

A study of the first 120 people to be supported by the ISS shows the following results. 38% were referrals to support hospital discharge and 62% were referrals from the community.

Reduced length of stay in hospital **26**

Prevented admission to hospital **12**

Reduced package of care **18**

Prevented package of care **27**

Prevented admission to care home **7**

Reduced carer strain / prevented breakdown **10**

Prevented provision of equipment **16**

A wider cohort study indicates that the reablement group had significantly better outcomes for 30-day re-admissions and social care costs when comparing the change between one year prior to intervention and three months after intervention.

Further work will be conducted to assess the financial cost of the intervention in terms of staffing and care costs against any savings made through a reduction in future service use. Initial calculations from this cohort indicate that the additional cost of social care during the reablement period can be offset by reduced need following reablement.

Conclusion

We know that we are only just beginning on our journey to transform reablement in Somerset. However, what we have learnt and the outcomes we are achieving give us the confidence to continue to embed this new way of working across the county and importantly to work on resolving the constraints and system conditions that get in the way of achieving purpose.

To conclude, a Taunton GP / Local Medical Committee Medical Secretary said the following after recent successful involvement of the ISS team with one of his patients:

> *"The ISS approach is more than a breath of fresh air; it is potentially a storm to blow away established unhelpful working practices...*
>
> *The best way to make the new NHS work is to continue to build organic cross-disciplinary teams who are given autonomy to share professional skills to find the quickest answer to each patient's problems. This is a new way of thinking that could really make a difference."*

About the authors

Ann Anderson

Deputy Director of Strategic Development,
NHS Somerset
Tel: 01935 384000

Ann worked as an Occupational Therapist within the NHS for many years, practising in both acute and community settings, before moving to a senior NHS management role 12 years ago. She is currently leading a number of strategic programmes in Somerset including Long-term Conditions. Her work includes some exciting initiatives to support improved quality and outcomes for service users and their families with a focus on achieving efficiencies in the system and preventing unnecessary admissions to hospital. Ann has led a range of service redesign programmes within both children's and adult services, working across organisational boundaries, envisioning individuals and teams to embrace innovation and new models of care.

Fred Parkyn

Service Re-Design Manager, Adult Social Care,
Somerset County Council.
Tel: 01823 355582

Fred qualified as a social worker and became a senior manager in Somerset County Council Adult social care with special responsibilities for liaison with the NHS. For the last 18 months, she has been working solely as the community services design manager and the project lead for adult social care on this project. She retires shortly.

7. HELPING PEOPLE SOLVE LEGAL AND SOCIAL WELFARE PROBLEMS

A CASE STUDY FROM NOTTINGHAM

Simon Johnson,
BOLD Advice Project Coordinator, AdviceUK

This case study illustrates the following:

- The consequences of system failure for citizens are stressful and can include homelessness and action by bailiffs to seize goods.

- Designing the 'fix' around what matters to customers keeps the citizen at the heart of the process and retains focus on achieving purpose.

- The importance of dialogue. The value of regular and ongoing discussions is that people involved 'in the work' and the leaders who own the system are actively learning about what matters, what works, and what makes a difference

- Working to purpose can bring dramatic results, in both service quality and reduced cost.

AdviceUK

AdviceUK is a charity supporting community organisations which give free advice to members of the public on legal and social welfare problems; for example, with debt, housing, benefits or employment.

Our 850 member organisations work in some of the poorest parts of the UK where, for over 2 million poor, marginalised, vulnerable and desperate people each year they are a trusted source of practical information, help and advocacy. People seek help from our member organisations when the state or the private sector lets them down and they don't get the benefits they're entitled to, face unmanageable debts or risk losing their home.

Since 2009, AdviceUK and Vanguard have supported an intervention to look at advice services in Nottingham, and have been working with

Nottingham City Council and the seven voluntary sector providers of advice that form the Advice Nottingham consortium.

Nottingham City Council

Nottingham City Council is a unitary authority, which has adopted an 'early intervention' approach to addressing social issues for a number of years, and has experience of deploying the Vanguard Method, most notably in Revenues and Benefits. The authority manages an in-house advice service and provides significant funding to independent third sector advice agencies.

Nottingham advice centres

Advice centres in Nottingham have worked in an increasingly collaborative way in recent years and formalised their relationship into a consortium – Advice Nottingham – through which they have taken a strategic, collaborative approach to service development, funding and delivery.

A shared ambition

Nottingham City Council and Advice Nottingham have built a close working relationship in recent years. In 2009, they began a shared review of advice provision using the Vanguard Method. The purpose of the review was:

- To design advice services in Nottingham around the needs of clients
- To commission client-centred and responsive advice services
- To work together in a coordinated way.

How the problem presented itself

Demand for advice has risen to record levels since the start of the economic crisis in 2008. 78% of AdviceUK members report[5] that demand has increased by 10% or more in the last 12 months. Research for the Money Advice Trust[6] showed that, in 2009, some 1.62 million people sought debt advice from a voluntary advice service, an increase of 350,000 on

---

5 Online member survey, December 2011

6 See http://bit.ly/Hc7fta

the previous year, and that every 1% increase in the International Labour Organisation measure of unemployment is associated with an additional 60,000 debt enquiries per quarter. Demand far outstrips supply: Pleasance *et al* (2010)[7] found that 36% of the UK population had a civil justice problem but that less than half of respondents managed to access advice.

Since the inception of the government's deficit reduction plan, pressure on funding for advice has increased. With local authorities as a primary source of income, independent advice providers are far from immune to the squeeze on the public purse. In 2011, 95% of AdviceUK members reported cuts in funding averaging £34,000 and were anticipating deeper cuts in the next financial year. 70% were cutting services. But these are not simple problems of resources or supply and demand. The capacity of advice services is limited significantly by two factors:

- The levels of systemic failure in public service administration which drive preventable demand into advice organisations and result in advisers having to take on casework to help clients to navigate the complexity of the system successfully. Advisers themselves also face the same repeated failures, taking up further capacity.

- The increasing shift in recent years from grant funding of advice to competitive procurement has exacerbated the pressure on advice services, by focusing on productivity targets that measure the volume of transactions delivered. AdviceUK has shown in earlier research[8] the unintended consequences of this approach. These include:

    - cherry-picking the least complex cases so they can be processed quickly to hit activity targets

    - closing cases as quickly as possible means the agency can trigger payment, but risks creating a revolving door for clients whose problems are not fully resolved

    - the pressure to deliver transactions reduces the scope for providers to address the demand for advice by working preventatively, and locks waste and cost into the system.

---

7 http://www.justice.gov.uk/downloads/publications/research-and-analysis/lsrc/2010CSJSAnnualReport.pdf

8 *It's the System Stupid! Radically Rethinking Advice,* AdviceUK, (2008)

So we wanted to explore a different approach to improving advice services – a bottom-up approach that others could adopt as an alternative to the untested, top-down prescriptions that are repeatedly handed down by governments.

The consequences of traditional work design

The way that work is traditionally designed requires the people in the system to focus on processing transactions, not solving problems and, without a clear understanding of what matters to customers and the purpose of the services, the inevitable result is more work, delays and poorer outcomes.

Advice Services

People rarely seek advice for simple single issues. Given the complex web of public services that people face when they lose their job, fall ill or have an accident, or their relationship breaks down, they bring multiple problems to advice organisations, and often at a late stage. Many people find it difficult to pick their way through the maze of lengthy application forms, remote customer contact centres and faceless processing factories and will often give up trying, so missing out on vital support, including income to which they are entitled.

When someone contacts an advice centre, an adviser will carry out a diagnostic interview and identify the range of issues to be addressed. These advisers may have the necessary expertise and experience to help or they may need to involve other colleagues or agencies. They will explore options with the client and agree a plan to address the problem. The adviser will normally open a case and initiate correspondence with the range of agencies involved to verify what has happened and open negotiations to put things right — often enlightening public officials as to their duties under the law or the flexibility available to them to do the right thing.

Cases can be 'live' for several months, with endless correspondence, progress-chasing, advocacy and negotiation. Hurdles include the difficulty of reaching the people who can solve the problems, as more and more processing centres are used to deliver public services. Those who can solve problems are 'protected' behind less experienced call handlers who are unable to answer substantive enquiries. Standard, scripted responses lead to errors and inflexibility and case ownership has disappeared, making it impossible to build a relationship that would solve problems quickly.

The casework approach adopted by advice workers can exacerbate the problems faced by the benefits service. In the pilot, we quickly discovered that advisers' interventions just add to the deluge of correspondence and enquiries faced by hard-pressed processing staff, adding further to the delays experienced by all their customers.

The local authority benefits service

For a local authority benefits service, the complexity of people's lives is also a major problem. Many customers move in and out of insecure or casual employment, resulting in repeated changes of circumstances. For those out of work, the service is reliant on claims information from the Department for Work and Pensions (DWP), which can cause delays and errors, particularly when benefit is suspended and then reinstated. A major system condition is the nationally available benefits IT system, which generates decision letters that drive significant amounts of failure demand. These cause major confusion for citizens and in many cases are simply binned as they make no sense to the layperson – even experienced advice workers find them difficult to interpret.

From the citizen's point of view

The consequences for individual citizens, trying to make sense of it all, often in desperate situations, can be huge:

- Delays in paying benefits can lead to people losing their homes because rent arrears is a mandatory ground for repossession for private tenants

- Arrears collection for Council Tax can be hugely traumatic for someone without the means to pay. Whilst recovery action should be suspended if there are benefit arrears, cases slip through the net, leaving people to face bailiffs threatening to seize goods to repay the 'debt'

- There is significant evidence of the link between a negative impact on an individual's health and wellbeing and the sort of financial problems caused by delays in benefit payments

- Delays in Council Tax payment result in additional enforcement costs for the citizen, which, if the result of benefit delays, are then refunded (with a further cost to the taxpayer).

Check

A team made up of staff from advice organisations across Nottingham carried out an initial piece of analysis to find out more about the demand being presented to advice organisations. Advisers doubled up with an adviser from another provider and, together, they recorded what clients said verbatim. They looked at a sample of 500 demands in total. The analysis showed that 30% of the demand is driven by the failure of public services to get something right for their customers.

Name of Agency	% of Failure Demands	% of Demand on Advice Services
DWP/ Job Centre Plus	25.00	7.63
Council Tax Collection	11.84	3.61
Housing Benefit	10.53	3.21
Nottingham City Homes	7.89	2.41
HM Revenues and Customs	5.26	1.61
Homelessness Service	3.29	1.00
Other Housing Associations	3.29	1.00
Utilities	3.29	1.00
Pensions Service	1.97	0.60
UK Border Agency	1.97	0.60
Council Tax Benefit	1.97	0.60
Adult Social Care	1.97	0.60
Child Support Agency	1.32	0.40
DVLA	0.66	0.20
Court Service	0.66	0.20
Other	9.87	3.01
None identified	9.21	2.81
TOTAL	100	30.52

Table 1: Type of Demand from Advice Organisations

The costs of failure demand

Additional research which we had commissioned from the New Economics Foundation (nef) helped us identify the financial implications of this failure. Nef calculated the cost of failure demands using a Social Return on Investment approach[9]. Costs were calculated both for the individual and their household (defined as social cost) and for the state.

Social costs capture some of the detrimental effects of problems that the individual or their family has to bear, such as debt interest charges, loss of home and costs of relocation, but also factors such as the negative impact on children, employment opportunities, or levels of stress.

Costs to the state arise when people's problems force them to turn to other public services. This might include, for instance, the cost to the public purse of more people going to their GP or being prescribed anti-depressants because of the stress of debt or homelessness.

Table 2 shows typical examples of over 30 interviews conducted.with an analysis of these hidden costs:

Case study	Social Cost	Cost to State	Total Cost
Debt – late intervention	£19,207	£9,511	£28,718
Debt – early intervention	£7,746	£1,521	£9,267
Housing – late intervention	£8,837	£5,287	£14,124
Housing – early intervention	£1,516	-	£1,516

Table 2: Analysis of Hidden Costs

This shows the huge potential for costs to be reduced by early intervention, both for the state and the individual. However, we wanted to find out if cost savings could be even greater when advice organisations and public services work together to identify and remove the preventable system failures.

---

9 *Outcomes in Advice,* AdviceUK (2010) contains the full research and an explanation of how Social Return on Investment normally works and how the method was adapted to cost failure. http://bit.ly/HaoCQw

Redesign

Our initial pilot involved two advice centres: Nottingham Law Centre and Bestwood Advice Centre, as well as Nottingham City Council's Housing and Council Tax Benefits Service. In setting up the work, we agreed the following aims:

- Understand the demand hitting the system and design a service that meets the needs of the customer.

- Jointly agree the purpose of the system and establish better measures to enable both organisations to understand their capability to deliver what matters to the customer.

- Increase the capacity of advice and benefits services by removing the causes of failure demand and reducing the waste steps.

- Demonstrate a way of working that could be used to support improvement in other services, in particular the key government agencies whose services impact on advice clients.

This case study focuses on the learning from the work that took place between March and May 2011.

Testing a new approach

The pilot team comprised three advisers in two advice centres, an experienced council benefits officer and the managers of both services, working with support from AdviceUK and Vanguard. Based on our learning from 'Check' in the advice sector, we set up a collaborative way of handling Housing Benefit (HB) or Council Tax Benefit (CTB) claims in advice centres. The pilot team took both new cases presented to the advice centres as well as some existing claims which were still being processed or where a problem had arisen.

Traditionally, when someone seeks help from an advice centre about HB or CTB, they are advised to go to the council and make a claim. When someone has a problem with an existing claim, the adviser contacts the council's benefits service to negotiate on their client's behalf.

However, the adviser doesn't have the power to solve the problem, only the council benefits team can do that, so, in the pilot, the adviser's role was changed fundamentally. Rather than advocate and negotiate from a distance, a pilot adviser contacts the benefits officer to discuss the merits of the case while the client is still with them. During the call, the benefits officer agrees a convenient time to meet the client and advises them about what information is needed to reach a decision. The adviser then explains the process to the client so s/he knows exactly where to go and what to do, and gives them a checklist showing all the information and evidence they need to take with them.

As the pilot progressed, we found that problems with existing claims can often be resolved without an interview, simply on the basis of the initial telephone contact, because the council has the information they need on their system. When an interview is required, the benefits officer assesses the claim and, in most cases, makes an immediate decision. We found that, by having established a relationship with the client, if the benefits officer needs additional information from them, they invariably bring it in without further chasing.

Crucially, once the benefits officer has made a decision, she explains it to the client and confirms it in writing in clear, everyday terms, so the individual knows, for example, how much rent or Council Tax they still have to pay.

Collecting data

To ensure that the pilot team learned what worked, we collected data at the start of the pilot, which is listed in the table below. We would use this data later in the process to develop measures.

Data	Purpose of collecting it	How we collect it
Type of demand	This will help us understand: • Volumes in • Type of demand • If demand changes as clients move along the system	Verbatim demand (as expressed by the client/ customer) at advice centre and at benefits interview
Root cause of the demand	This will help us understand why people need help; e.g. long-term debt, unemployment, delays in other benefits, claims refused, etc.	This may need subtle questioning although it may emerge from general discussion

Data	Purpose of collecting it	How we collect it
% of demand that is referred to benefits officer	This will help us understand the relationship between the number of clients presenting for help v those that can/should be helped directly by Nottingham County Council	Daily count of number of clients presenting v those referred
Total adviser appointment time	This will help us understand capacity by demand type	Timed entry for each client that records actual time spent setting up clean*
% time benefits officer available when contacted by adviser	This will help us understand capacity	Daily count of times when not available
% time advisers available to deal with queries from benefits officer	This will help us to understand capacity	Daily count of times when advisers are contacted and not available
% of clients that are set-up clean by advisers	This will help us understand our capability to set cases up clean	Daily count of times when a client arrives for an appointment without all that is required, including what was missing
Time from adviser appt to first appt with benefits officer	This will help us understand capacity	Adviser records date referred and date of appointment made; benefits officer records any deviations from original appointment and reason

* Clean:ensuring they have all the information needed to resolve the issue.

Data	Purpose of collecting it	How we collect it
Total benefits appointment time	This will help us understand capacity by demand type	Timed entry for each client that records actual time spent at each appointment resolving issues
% of cases resolved at first appointment with benefits officer	This will help us to understand our capability to resolve cases at first point of contact and, if we can't, why not.	Record daily count of all issues resolved at first appointment and record reasons for those that could not be
Total end-to-end time to resolution	This will help us understand our capability to meet demand from initial contact to resolution	E-2-E time recorded by adviser and benefits officer as may be defined differently for each service
Number of tasks cleared from backlog at NCC	This will help us understand the relationship between not getting it right first time and NCC backlog level	Benefits officer to capture how many tasks are cleared from backlog

Table 3: Collecting Data

During the pilot period, the team met weekly and reviewed the cases that had been handled and what the demands and data showed. We maintained an Issues and Blockages Log, so we could keep track of problems that arose, either with the new way of working or more generally. Responsibility was allocated for problem-solving and progress followed up at the weekly meetings. This process of learning from each other and understanding and implementing what worked to meet client demand was crucial.

At the end of 10 weeks, we met to collate the data and explore what had been learnt overall.

Nominal value and failure demand

We analysed verbatim demands that had been recorded at both the advice agencies and at the benefits service. The pilot team agreed they represented the nominal demands represented in Table 4.

Advice Services	%	
I want some advice	0%	
What am I entitled to?	9%	
Help me claim	6%	
My circumstances have changed	19%	
I've claimed: what's happening?	16%	**Total Preventable Demand**
I don't understand	19%	
I want to challenge / appeal	3%	
Help me sort it out	28%	**66%**
TOTAL	**100%**	
NCC Benefits Service	**%**	
What am I entitled to?	4%	
I want to claim	20%	
Backdate my claim	6%	
My circumstances have changed	9%	
When will you assess my claim?	19%	**Total Preventable Demand**
What's happened [about my claim]?	9%	
I don't understand	19%	
How have you made your decision?	6%	**60%**
I want to challenge / appeal	7%	
Please reduce the overpayment recovery rate	2%	
TOTAL	**100%**	

*Table 4: Nominal demand presented to advice services
and NCC Benefits Service*

The pilot team agreed that the highlighted demands were preventable – predictably around 60%. An ideal service would make clear, correct decisions quickly and communicate them in a way that customers can understand.

A new purpose

Based on the analysis of demand and on an assessment of what matters to customers, the team agreed the following purpose for services working in the pilot:

"Help me pay my rent and Council Tax by making a decision and paying my benefit quickly"

By designing work together, to deliver what matters to customers, the focus has moved towards achieving an overall purpose of helping people pay their liabilities, rather than completing individual transactions.

Working to purpose for the benefits service means that when staff interact with customers they don't just deal with the presenting problem but aim to resolve the claim and ensure that customers understand what is happening.

In the case of advice services, as the adviser is not able to solve the problem their client faces, the pilot has involved a change in role from *"provide advice and advocacy"* to *"set the claim up 'clean' and get the client to the person who can solve their problem as quickly as possible"*.

Designing services using the Vanguard Method normally involves trying to eliminate 'hand-offs', i.e. where a piece of work is 'handed off' from one person or service to another. However, in this case a hand-off from the advice service to a benefits officer is the right thing to do to solve the problem. The aim is then to make the hand-off 'clean', in other words, to ensure the benefits officer has all the information they need to resolve the issue.

This represents a fundamental shift in work design from traditional case management, and we learned that working to purpose in this way creates a significant amount of additional capacity.

Comparing the pilot with the existing system

The review team mapped the flow of work for typical cases, to identify the number of steps taken, those steps that add value to meeting customer demand and those that represent waste.

		Existing system		Pilot
		Case 1	Case 2	Case 1
End-to-end time (days)		160	98	6
Steps				
Advice service	Value	2	2	1
	Waste	8	6	6
Benefits service	Value	7	5	8
	Waste	10	12	2
Total steps	Value	9	7	9
	Waste	18	18	8

Table 5: High-Level Flow Comparative Data

The reduction in waste steps in both services, most notably in the benefits service, demonstrates the potential to release capacity in the system by adopting this method of working.

Figure 1 below shows the high-level flows for two cases from the existing system and Figure 2 shows the flow of work for a pilot case.

Key to both Figures:

- Grey shapes indicate waste steps
- Clear shapes indicate value steps
- Steps in square boxes are undertaken by the advice agency
- Steps in circles are undertaken by the NCC's Benefits Service

CIS: Customer Service System

RB Live: Revenue and Benefits System

O/P: over payment

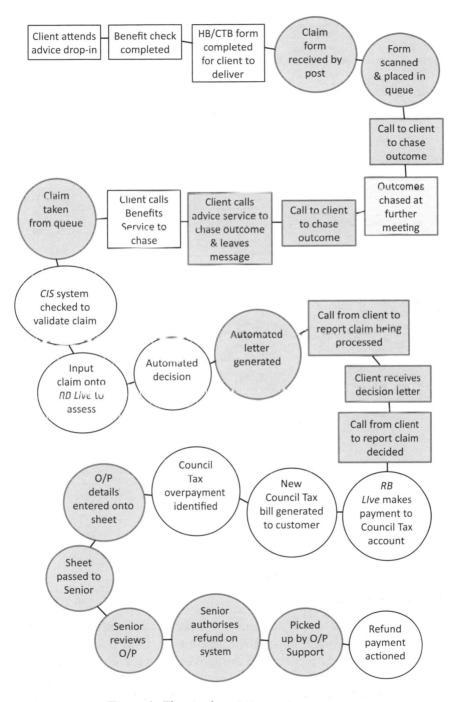

Figure 1: Flow in the existing system

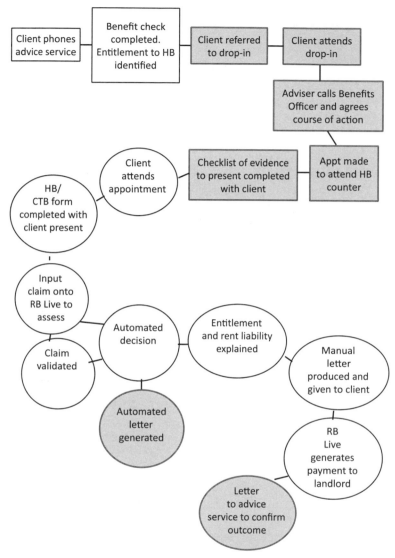

Figure 2: Pilot flow

End-to-end times

Given that what matters to customers is to receive a speedy decision and payment to enable them to pay their liabilities, the time taken to resolve cases is an important measure. In the above examples, end-to-end times were reduced from 160 and 98 days to 6 days. This finding was validated by comparing the end-to-end times for all pilot cases against those for a sample of 18 cases from the old system. When the data is plotted into capability charts (Figure 3) the impact is dramatic. The first section of the graph is from the old system, in which the mean end-to-end time was 100 days. In the early stages of the pilot, the mean end-to-end time was reduced to 23 days, and by the end of the pilot, as systems bedded in and those involved became used to the new ways of working, it had fallen to 5 days. This reduction in time taken to process cases clearly has a dramatic impact on the service the customer receives, but also on the potential to increase the capacity of staff working in the system.

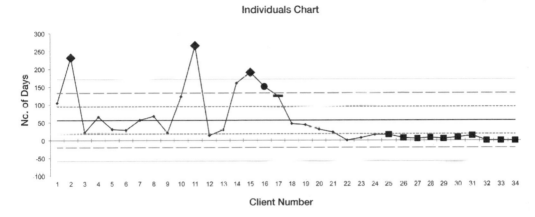

Figure 3: Data showing end-to-end times for individual cases

Results

Traditional ways of working can cause huge delays for people in receiving the benefits to which they are entitled, and this can threaten their home and goods. These delays also lead to significant stress for the citizen and their family. The complexity of the system feels impenetrable, especially for people for whom English is not their first language.

One advice centre client said they now had confidence in the council for the first time in a very long time. Another summed up the reaction of many people using the pilot service.

> *"I can't believe how quickly this was sorted out. It was all done on the same day – that's never happened before. You were both brilliant, thanks."*

In one case that was brought into the pilot from the old system, when the advice agency contacted their client's landlord to inform him of the outcome of the HB claim, he said he had not believed his tenant had really made a claim as [under the old system] it was taking so long. As soon as he heard the outcome he withdrew possession action. In another example, a tenant had been in dispute for months over repairs. The speedy resolution of the benefit claim through the pilot cleared her rent arrears, and the landlord put right the disrepair in the property.

These responses were supported by advisers. Nick Mathisson from Nottingham Law Centre said:

> *"The experience of working in this way has been almost entirely a positive one. Our clients are often coming to us as a last resort for dealing with their problems. It has undoubtedly kept clients in their homes and made a massive, positive difference."*

This was echoed by Nick's colleague, Safoora Khatoon:

> *"The change is amazing. Cases that would have taken 4 - 6 months can be dealt with so promptly."*

Overall, advisers estimated that 18% of the cases would typically have taken months to resolve in the old system, given the complexity of the issues, with immense consequences for their clients. With the new way of working, they were all resolved in days.

The shorter resolution times have had an impact on capacity and cost. AdviceUK has commissioned an independent evaluation, including an economic analysis of the work in Nottingham, supported and funded by the Baring Foundation.

The evaluation shows that advice agencies were able to close pilot cases in ¼ of the time taken to resolve comparable cases through the traditional casework approach, and processing took less than ½ of the average number of adviser hours. Advice agency cases in the pilot were calculated to cost £77.40, compared with £166.96 for comparable cases in the previous system. Whilst robust cost data is not available from Nottingham City Council, the evaluation has shown that the typical length of time the benefits service takes to process a case is now 16 days, compared to 56 days for traditionally managed cases.

Next steps

A perfect benefits system would support people to pay their rent and Council Tax by always making decisions and paying benefit quickly, without the need for customers to turn to advice services. Given that it will take time to address the complexity within the benefits system, the role of advice in helping people to access their entitlements is essential.

Nottingham City Council and Advice Nottingham have agreed that this way of working should be scaled up and applied across other advice agencies in the city. Two more agencies were rolled-in to the new way of working over the summer of 2011 and, at the time of writing, the benefits service is in the process of scaling up the approach internally, to engage the remaining advice providers who manage higher volumes.

The following measures have been agreed, to make sure the services carry on learning:

Leading Measures

- End-to-end times from presentation to resolution
- The number of touches required to resolve.

Lagging Measures

- The number of call attempts required to hand-off to the Benefits Service

Further interventions

AdviceUK and Vanguard have since supported a further intervention in another location, enabling us to use what we learned in Nottingham. In this second intervention, we have also supported the local authority to re-commission its advice services in a more intelligent way. This has important implications for the future design and commissioning of independent advice services.

Intelligent commissioning

A major system condition that stops advice organisations working in a preventative way is the drive towards competitive procurement, based on top-down specifications that focus on increased 'productivity', in the flawed belief that delivering a higher volume of work is a good thing. This focus on productivity means that commissioners reduce their ability to tackle the causes of demand and achieve real value.

However, in this second pilot, advice services have been commissioned to a simple purpose, based on an analysis of client demand and what matters to people who use advice services: "Help local people to solve their problems". Providers have been given a number of principles to work to, key to which is collaboration to address the drivers of demand, by working with public service organisations and other agencies in the city. The means of delivery are not specified, enabling the successful bidder to design a service that will meet its purpose.

The measures by which the new service will be assessed are not about the volume of transactions supplied but about the type and level of demand, and reducing levels of demand – especially failure demand. This incentivises the provider to operate in a preventative way, both to collaborate with public services to help them minimise failure but also to address underlying causes, such as unemployment or individuals' poor financial capability.

Conclusion

It is no exaggeration to say that advice services face a real crisis. Escalating demand and reduced funding mean that people with problems are likely to find it harder to access the services they need to help them solve their problems. As market-based competition is introduced as the default option for commissioning services, the pressure on advice organisations to process more and more transactions will only increase. As AdviceUK's work has shown, this pressure incentivises services to do the wrong thing, reduces quality and choice, and locks waste and cost into the system.

Our work in Nottingham has shown the potential of a different approach: an approach that focuses on cooperation to tackle the causes of people seeking advice, resulting in improved services and lower costs.

But the real impact – the real benefit of this approach – is on the members of the public who currently try to navigate an impenetrable benefits system and meet delay, miscommunication and error. If we can help public services improve what they do, then some of the poorest members of the community will benefit from services that really help and support them to achieve greater independence and a more sustainable future.

About the Author

Simon Johnson
Email: simon.johnson@adviceuk.org.uk
Mobile: 07960 790946
Web: www.adviceuk.org.uk/bold

Simon has worked for AdviceUK since May 2009 and coordinates BOLD, a project that addresses concerns that the procurement of advice services based on top-down, target-driven specifications limits their potential to make a real difference.

Simon has worked in the voluntary sector since 1985, with extensive involvement in a number of cross-sector partnership activities.

8. IMPROVED STROKE CARE AT HALF THE COST

Dr Steve Allder,
Consultant Neurologist, Plymouth Hospital Trust

This case study illustrates the following:

- Clinical evidence in a health setting makes a powerful case for change.

- Understanding and designing to meet high variety demand in service organisations reduces costs.

- If you think you have a problem with rising demand for your service, study it. You may find demand is actually stable.

- Redesigning existing work based on rigorous experiment and iteration is more effective than making major change based on a pre-determined plan.

- An empirically based, bottom-up design for improvement with a secure mandate from an executive team had no problems of 'buy-in'.

Introduction

This chapter is about improving the care for stroke patients in Plymouth.

Plymouth Hospitals NHS Trust (PHT) is a large hospital with 56 stroke beds across two specialist stroke units.

In England, strokes are a major health problem. Every year over 150,000 people have a stroke. It is the third largest cause of death after heart disease and cancer. The brain damage caused by strokes means that they are the largest cause of adult disability in the UK.

Central to stroke care is the concept of a 'pathway'. Pathways are designed to reduce unnecessary variations in patient care when the clinical course of the condition is predictable. More than just a guideline or a protocol, a care pathway is typically a single all-encompassing bedside document that stands as an indicator of the care a patient is likely to be provided. It is also a single unified legal record of the care the patient has received and the progress of their condition. Variations from the pathway may occur as clinical freedom is exercised to meet the needs of the individual patient.

Many different individuals and providers are involved in the care and rehabilitation of stroke patients. For example, a stroke patient may need help from a team of specially trained nurses, surgeons, radiographers, specialist consultants, physiotherapists, speech therapists and social workers.

Connection with Vanguard

I have been interested in management, leadership and clinical system improvements since becoming a consultant in 2003. My development as a practitioner and leader has been supported via programmes with the National Institute for Innovation and the Health Foundation.

My interest in systems and innovation led me to read John Seddon's book *Freedom from Command and Control* (2003). His description of capability charts applied to a housing context taught me something new. I learnt that understanding demand is a prerequisite for improving and innovating in service systems.

Why we started the work

At PHT, stroke mortality rose by 3% between 1997 and 2008/09. The Trust had the highest stroke mortality in the region in 2008/09. Although demand for stroke services at PHT had been consistent at 547 admissions per year, bed occupancy and the Average Length of Stay (ALOS) had been variable. This suggested that the challenge was not excess demand but rather how services were being delivered. The high variability in length of stay was contributing to a spending deficit of £2,000 per patient.

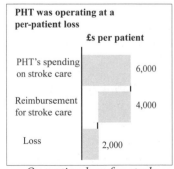

*Operating loss for stroke
care patients*

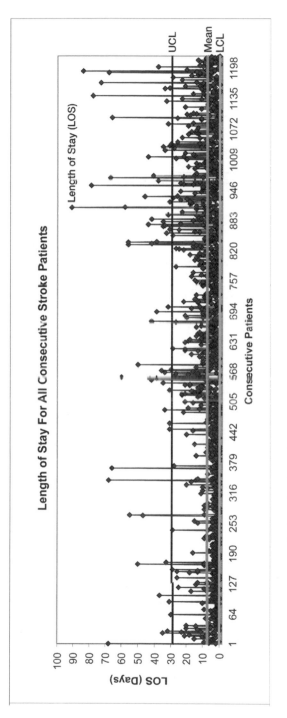

The length of stay for stroke patients was high and highly variable.

Stroke care became a strategic priority following the publication of the National Stroke Strategy in mid-2008 and the development of the Strategic Health Authority's Improvement Plan. This signalled an imperative to improve and resources to support this to happen.

However, there were divergent views amongst clinical members about how to approach the change. Four solutions were considered to address the high variability of ALOS for stroke patients and the resulting per-patient loss.

Suggested Solution	Challenge	
Build a larger stroke unit in the PHT to ensure that all targets are met	• Requires more beds for an entire ward which is higher cost • Wouldn't necessarily provide evidence-based care	More costly given need for greater resources; not backed by evidence.
Provide early supportive discharge with enhanced therapy in Care Homes via hospital teams	• Reduce bed occupancy • Lack of pathway approach causes a gap in understanding community support needs, causing difficulty in accurately resourcing community support.	Do not address the fact that the problem is not demand but the way in which the supply of services is managed.
Provide all onward care from hospital	• Leads to duplication of services since primary care trusts already provide comunity care • Triggering unnecessary competition	
Redesign existing pathway	• Identify ways to deliver high-quality care within given cost constrains • Design an integrated pathway with a view of entire care setting	
Rigorous evidence was used to change the widely accepted idea that more resources were needed.		

Because other considered solutions were more costly and not backed by evidence, the solution was to redesign the existing pathway.

Given the financial reality in the organisations involved, substantial further investment was not viable so my proposal to achieve the improvements in care at the same or less cost was finally approved. Establishing who would be accountable and responsible for the pathway performance was a very stressful process because the pathway involved several different providers. This meant the mandate needed executive sign-off from the Acute Trust and the PCT provider arm. However, once approved, I was able to introduce a simple, clear structure, and as a leadership team we spent considerable effort ensuring everyone was clear about their role.

The health community already had large amounts of data relating to the existing Stroke Pathway. This was collated and presented in more readily understandable formats, and we made it clear through the new structure that all of the ongoing management and change should be based on these new data dashboards[10]. Achieving buy-in as the work progressed was relatively simple because the dashboards showed clear areas of opportunity.

Check

Our analysis of demand coming into the Stroke Unit revealed that for as long as we had been collecting demand figures (more than 10 years), demand was extremely stable. The average number of admissions of stroke patients was 1.5 per day over two years, and this varied from 0-5.

Understanding what matters

Our starting point was to determine what patients really needed from the Stroke Pathway. We considered diagnosis, acute treatment, secondary prevention (treatment that stops it from happening again), avoiding medical complications, and obtaining optimal functional stability (getting back on your feet or feeling well enough to leave an acute hospital). From this it was clear that, while there were opportunities to improve each element, getting people back on their feet and feeling well enough to leave hospital was the area we needed to focus on. We had been collecting data relating to this over the previous 3-4 years and so were now able to specifically dissect what this was telling us. Our audits showed us that not getting this right was one of the main causes of variability in the patient's length of stay.

---

10 A 'Clinical Dashboard' is a toolset of visual displays developed to provide clinicians with the relevant and timely information they need to inform daily decisions that improve quality of patient care. http://bit.ly/GNtZjJ

Data on 'status pre-stroke' and 'clinical size of stroke' also showed us very clearly that we had not designed an appropriate pathway of care for patients who were frail prior to their stroke and had a severe new stroke.

This group was also consuming a large, highly variable number of beds day-to-day which was making running the unit complex and also contributing to the poor financial position.

Preferred place of discharge for 6 subgroups of patients (percentage of total)			
Clinical stroke size			
Patient status pre-stroke	**Mild**	**Moderate**	**Severe**
Frail**	RSU* or convalescence	RSU or convalescence (20%)	Pathway redesign required (16%)
Well	Home (23%)	RSU (13%)	RSU (11%)

* Rehabilitation Stroke Unit
** Frail patients were defined as having a medical complexity index of 3,4 or 5 on a 1-5 scale. 0 = no systemic disease other than primary diagnosis; 1 = premorbid, inactive or irrelevant systemic disease; 2 = active systemic disease not limiting function; 3 = active systemic disease limiting function; 4 = active systemic disease severely limiting function, 5= moribund terminal state.

Redesign

The team reviewed a consecutive batch of patient notes relating to the frail patient with a severe stroke. They concluded it would not be possible to develop a clear-cut protocol for every patient, but by identifying this group of patients and collecting a pre-defined set of data, it should be possible to manage the patients along what was termed the 'expectant pathway'. For the remainder of the patients the team simply reviewed established guidelines and protocols. These appeared evidence-based and fit for purpose so no changes were made.

A completely new expectant pathway (below) designed to get frail patients with severe strokes well enough to leave the acute hospital became the focus of our improvement work.

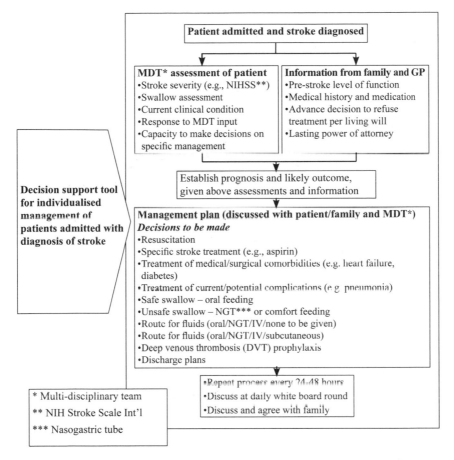

*Current Draft of the End-to-End Pathway for frail patients with
severe strokes, which includes metrics, value-added activities and
decision rights*

In under a year, access to and use of the Stroke Unit became more efficient. The time taken to transfer patients from the emergency department to the Acute Stroke Unit fell by 12% between April 2009 and February 2010 and the average length of stay (LOS) dropped by 6% over the same period. The percentage of patients spending at least 90% of their time in the Acute Stroke Unit rose by 7%.

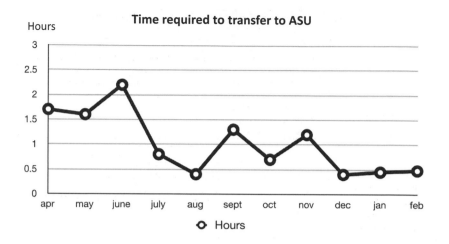

Figure 1: Time taken to transfer patient from emergency to ASU

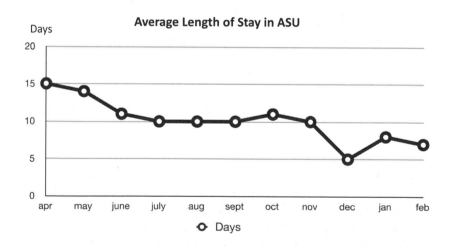

Figure 2: Length of stay (LOS) in ASU.

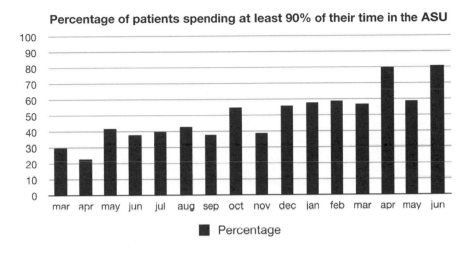

Percentage of patients spending at least 90% of their time in the ASU

The next phase of the project was to make sure there was a clear expectation of how we wanted local teams to use the pathway and associated data. After 4 weeks of giving the local teams space and autonomy it became clear that they were not able to achieve what we were hoping they would. As a consequence, the leadership team started to attend local team meetings and provide a role model of what we were asking them to do by going to the ward and showing them. Within two months the teams had a better understanding of what we were saying and what this meant in reality. They then became more than capable of delivering the changes themselves.

With the new structure embedded we went to great lengths to find areas of improvement and to praise individuals who had particularly championed change. We actively visited teams and identified those people within them who were showing a particular aptitude for taking management and leadership positions and we encouraged them to carry out small projects within their area. It is intended that these people will be invited to leadership development days, with a view to creating a sustainable pipeline of leaders and managers within this clinical service.

We have not had to put in any additional resource or guidelines at a local team level. Simply asking and empowering local teams to manage to their own guidelines, while using their own establishments, has delivered the improvements shown in the charts above.

Measures

The improvements in the Stroke Unit were driven through the weekly 'within-unit' meeting. Because the patient pathways extend beyond the Stroke Unit, improvements across the broader pathways were managed through a 'Pathway Provider' meeting and measured via a complementary set of operational measures. Through this process it was possible to create improvement in discrete elements of the pathway, and coordinate improvement between elements where the data suggested joined-up improvement work was possible. For example, the 24-hour thrombolysis coverage for patients was trialled and embedded as a result of this process.

Changes were tested and monitored by the teams within and across the pathway. This not only produced significant measurable improvement, it also created a supportive and exciting environment in which to provide care and service improvement.

To measure the impact of the new pathway, the team developed a dashboard of relevant operational metrics that was updated daily by a dedicated data analyst. This data was reviewed in a weekly meeting and areas where we were failing to achieve our goals were further examined and potential solutions proposed and trialled. This approach enabled significant improvements in multiple measures to be achieved.

It is important to note that the National Stroke Strategy and the Strategic Health Authority developed their own set of targets and measures. Our approach recognised the importance of reporting on these measures. However, the development of local metrics was based on an analysis of our work in reality. This approach was successful. We achieved all the national targets that we were expected to report on by default.

Leadership

This project was greatly enhanced by the Pathway Provider group leadership team emerging from an existing team within the Acute Trust. Where the team evolved from was far less important that the composition of the team. Each of the team members had a good grounding in different elements, e.g. the need for careful empirical analysis, the need for great care in understanding how to motivate local teams and pathway cooperation, and the importance of on-the-ground delivery from the existing teams.

At the start of the process there was significant distrust and explicit hostility from different teams within the patient pathway. However, because the mandate was securely established from the executive teams across the health economy, local teams engaged with the process. The process was empowering, bottom-up and empirically based which meant that achieving and maintaining clinical buy-in has not been a problem at any point. In fact the Commissioner accountable for the Stroke Pathway commented after 6 months that she couldn't believe, given the hostility at the beginning of the process, that the changes achieved had been so significant with so little audible dissent.

Summary of results

- Initial feedback from relatives indicates that they are more satisfied with patient care.

- The number of patients receiving CT scans within 24 hours has increased by 91%.

- Within one year (2009-2010), access to and use of the Acute Stroke Unit has become more efficient.

- The time required for transfer to ASU decreased 12%.

- The percentage of stroke patients who spend ≥90% of their time in the Acute Stroke Unit increased 7%.

- 100% of patients are now assessed for thrombolysis.

- 100% of patients undergo a swallow screen within 24 hours.

Savings

In just under 3 months, the initiative enabled the Plymouth Hospitals Trust to save an average of £1,000 per stroke patient and to close 17 beds.

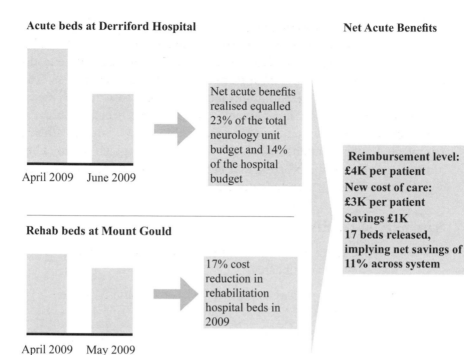

Acute beds at Derriford Hospital

April 2009   June 2009

Net acute benefits realised equalled 23% of the total neurology unit budget and 14% of the hospital budget

Net Acute Benefits

 **Reimbursement level:
£4K per patient
New cost of care:
£3K per patient
Savings £1K
17 beds released,
implying net savings of
11% across system**

Rehab beds at Mount Gould

17% cost reduction in rehabilitation hospital beds in 2009

April 2009   May 2009

Key success factors

- Clinical leadership supported by clinical evidence behind the case for change

- Operational and analytical rigour when implementing change to ensure performance

- Willingness to take risks when supported by evidence

- Focus on holistic pathway rather than individual elements

Conclusion

On the 18th of June 2010 the Strategic Health Authority team that had visited two years earlier came to make a new evaluation. Their initial evaluation had been damning. They found a clinical pathway that was disjointed, providing patchy, low-quality care. When they returned it was possible to present to them a joined-up clinical pathway articulated via 8 local teams, united by one single purpose: optimising the care of patients of stroke from the moment they had clinical symptoms, back into the community and beyond. It was the most satisfying experience I have had in my career as a clinician and clinical manager.

One Ward Manager said:

> *"I used to spend most of my time in meetings with distressed relatives. I don't have to any more because we get things right. I can now get on with my job."*

A Consultant said:

> *"We now have time to talk to each other, human to human. What a change."*

Any acute provider could lead a similar transformation. The core premise of this initiative is improving the efficiency of current operations. Management should have a clearly defined focus and scope in order to facilitate operational improvements among front-line workers.

About the author

Dr Steven Allder
Tel: 0845 155 8155/01752 202082

Plymouth Hospitals NHS Trust
Derriford Road
Crownhill
Plymouth
Devon
PL6 8DH

Steve Allder is a consultant neurologist and Clinical Director for the Stroke Service Line at Plymouth Hospitals Trust. His sub-specialist interest is acute stroke. He has been interested in management, leadership and clinical system improvements since becoming consultant in 2003. He's had experience as a sub-specialist lead, a clinical director of neuroscience and ophthalmology, a clinical director of a cross-community stroke service line and, most recently, as assistant medical director of Plymouth Hospitals Trust.

PART TWO

9. UNDERSTANDING DEMAND

Richard Davis, Vanguard Consulting

Demand as the point of leverage

A distinguishing characteristic of the Vanguard Method is the focus on the notion of demand. In his book, *The Fifth Discipline*, Peter Senge notes that systems should be thought of as having points of leverage. We believe demand is the point of leverage in many systems.

Academics and others like to worry about definitions of terms and labels – it is their field – but for the practitioner the point-of-leverage label is very simply defined; it is the point at which you take action. If removing preventable demand makes a big difference to your capacity, you have probably started in the right place. The rest of your demand, therefore, should be the stuff that matters to your customers. If when you do exactly and only what matters to your customers all your indicators improve then demand was a good place to start.

The other merit of this logic is that it provides a linear model for understanding a system – there is a place to start and a logical sequence to follow. A complaint about many systems views is that they create complexity and make it difficult to know where to begin.

In demand-driven service systems (where demand is the best place to act) the key task is to understand the predictable variety of that demand and design your system against it. Many in the lean community maintain that 'pull' is irrelevant in service systems. From experience, however, it has been very helpful to us to view 'design against demand' as the equivalent of 'pull' in service.

As you look at your system and as you continue through this chapter keep that thought in mind: the knowledge required is to know where and how to act.

Mass production logic

Mass production logic, with efficiency at its core, has transactionalised services both in the public and private sector. This has resulted in high cost, low value service. For example, in the private sector, a financial services system will take a call from a customer, enter the perceived problem into the system and pass it on to a back office in the UK or anywhere in the world. This is deemed efficient, in that having dedicated call centres supposedly makes best use of people's time and expertise. It also appears to reduce the cost of calls and back office transactions. However, the result is that managers only know the cost performance of the call centre and the back office as separate entities. Yet the customer knows them as one entity. It will be certain that the organisation will have no data about how well they solve customers' problems or the total resource that is involved.

We worked in a telecoms organisation that scored 92% consistently on its key measure of first time problem resolution. Yet, because most calls required outsourcing to a repair organisation, very few calls could be resolved at first contact for the customer – by design!

So, even in relatively simple systems, the notion of demand must not be seen transactionally but from the customer's perspective in terms of what matters to them and what problem it is that they need you to solve.

In the public sector it is routinely more complex. For example, the health service measures how long it takes to diagnose cancer but the measure is rarely the true end-to-end time from the patient's perspective: initial GP appointment, to test, to GP, to test, to specialist, to test, to further test, to specialist, etc. Diagnosis can take — and often does take — months with no end-to-end knowledge gained. Again, this is no academic debate about 'labels' but a clear headed focus on the best way and the best place to intervene and act in order to make the most efficacious changes to the system.

Two important questions for managers

There are two important questions to consider:

1. What is the most useful way to view 'demand'?
2. What relationship do we want with our citizen?

These two questions are integral.

1. What is the most useful way to view demand?

Start with demand if you can quickly see that understanding types and patterns of contact will make a significant difference to your system (cutting out waste and improving service experience). The knowledge that you are seeking should, therefore be: 'what are the predictable causes of these patterns?'

An example: every January the calls received by local authorities about potholes peak. The council get calls telling them about potholes, telling them that the pothole is still there or telling them that a vehicle has been damaged. It also gets questions from the public about how to make a claim. Each of these will represent a strand of work. If we focus on whether we have dealt with the call well ('customer satisfaction') then the improvement work will focus on the processing of calls and claims. Does this improve the system? No, the same calls will come in when the next set of weather events does its worst.

A better way to study demand, in this case, is to view the roads as the cause of demand and to view the caller as someone we always do our best for but not as the 'demand'. Better questions to ask are: 'What do we know about the roads and their life condition?' 'What do we know about the causes of potholes?' Potholes are weather related, obviously, but also very strongly correlated with 'end of life roads' and utility works. Yet the system is designed to handle calls, meet insurance requirements, fulfil 'inspection schedules' and avoid negligence claims.

What should we pay attention to?

The better questions to ask yourself are: 'What knowledge and what perspective will drive the biggest improvements?' 'Do we pay attention to the state of the road and stronger enforcement/better contracts with utilities or do we pay attention to customer service standards?' Whilst the answer may appear obvious, it must be an empirical choice – experiment and find out.

One of the problems with the craze for Customer Relationship Management systems was that they led to collecting 'knowledge' about the callers and not about the true demand – the roads, the parks, the houses, etc. There is, then, a type of demand that will not vary whoever lives in a particular geographical area. It will be worth experimenting to discover the best way of describing and analysing that demand.

The Leicestershire Ambulance Service found that understanding demand by geography saved more lives than trying to improve response standards. Staffordshire Fire and Rescue has created huge improvement by looking at incidents by type and geography instead of by response standards and equipment standards.

Police forces have long known the role of 'location' but have been sidetracked by looking at demand as activity generated by callers. They are beginning to rediscover the importance of knowledge about the community, how much is down to key individuals and how much is the geography itself, whoever lives there. Policing also highlights a practical problem with understanding demand. The last 15 years have turned demand largely into 'something that comes in to the contact centre'. This is true for policing and the first option for learning about demand is to sit in the call centre. Demand, also, is *de facto* what is 'recorded'. What becomes obvious in practice, however, is that much of the true demand happens on the street where people talk to Police Community Support Officers and none of that is recorded or seen by the system. Indeed, the role of the contact centre in most organisations is to classify the 'demand' to fit the system even when that which is recorded is subject to systematic distortion.

One of the most unhelpful conversations to have is trying to define the 'customer' in identifying sources of demand. More, later, of why the word 'customer' is itself unhelpful but, depending on the perspective you choose, the 'customer' in any guise is often not the source of the demand that you would want to see. We want to know about the roads, the parks, the houses, the housing estates, etc. The caller is but one way of knowing about issues. It could be argued that all of this demand is 'failure' demand in that, if that fabric of our geography were to be kept in good condition, the caller demand would never arise.

The problem we are really trying to solve

An important task for the internal leader is, therefore, to find a helpful language that creates the right focus. Demand is a useful construct as the point of leverage for most service systems but it can be unhelpful in a practical sense in that it often connotes 'transactions' (e.g. calls) or activity/workload. You will find your own language but what we have found increasingly helpful is to talk about 'the problem we are really trying to solve'. 'The problem we are really trying to solve' is... how to keep the roads in good condition; how to keep a good quality housing stock; how to resolve the problems in the housing estate; how to prevent predictable fires, etc. So, 'if the road could talk, what would it tell us?' becomes the sort of knowledge you look for.

Not all demand is geographic. Much is also specific to individuals. People may need help to live the life they want to lead, to run a business, to be safe, to educate their children and so on.

Again, the challenge is for you to decide on the right/best problem to solve. The transactional demand – the call, the conversation – will, at best, be an indicator.

Hidden demand

A common 'demand' for local authorities is 'please put me on your housing list'. What would we learn if we had a proper conversation about the problem the person was trying to solve by going on the list? One authority tried this and the following were some of the reasons:

- My garden is too big for me and I'm struggling to look after it

- It's an insurance policy for when I get older

- My kids are 16 and it's time they left – give them a house

- We've just got married and got nowhere to live

- I'm homeless

So what is the problem we are trying to solve for these citizens? Is going on the housing list a solution? This authority realised that in more than 70% of cases, the housing list was no solution at all and it had the capability to provide better and cheaper solutions. (As a nation, we think we have a shortage of social housing. It's possible that we do but we currently don't know.)

A high demand for the police is 'missing persons'. They have a procedure for missing persons which comes into play every time one is logged. When you look at them one by one and ask what problem needs solving you see a very different picture. You will very rarely find what we would describe as a genuinely missing person. What you will find is:

- Care homes reporting people/children 'missing' to comply with their own risk procedures. The people are not 'missing', simply not back by the prescribed time. Or children who have been relocated and 'bunk off' to see their friends back home.

- People who 'abscond' from hospitals.

- Parents who cannot control their children and want the police to do it for them, 'go and bring him home – he won't listen to us'.

The health sector 'sees' and treats medical problems but many are social problems in disguise. Around 70% of unscheduled admissions to acute hospitals are entirely preventable (e.g. older people who call 999 because they are alone and panic). 20% of attendance at cottage hospitals is due to what doesn't work for the person at their GP surgery – not open, wrong diagnosis, part treatment, etc.

People who claim housing benefit could be simply processed as claimants. Underlying that, however, will be a range of problems around finance. What is interesting is that most people who attend Citizens Advice Bureaux and other welfare advice agencies have financial problems and have generally waited until they are in crisis before they seek help. This creates consequential demand that is often difficult to service on all sorts of systems: rent, debtors, credit agencies, banks, etc. More importantly, it is difficult to help the person out of the hole they are in, which means extended and repeat problems. The probability is that many such people will come first to the Housing Benefit team and at a time before they are in crisis. The way we choose to understand demand will determine the problem we choose to solve.

This logic has profound implications for public agencies. Success means 'design against demand'. How you choose to think about demand and what you learn when you do so will dictate the design of your service. The probability is that no agency is currently designed with an exclusive remit for the problems they will uncover.

A good example is the focus on 'chaotic families'. What you learn is that agencies have branded them 'problems' but offered little help; they often do not claim benefits and will have health and education problems. Who designs the help? Who measures the outcomes? Who carries the cost?

This now begs the second question:

2. What relationship do we want with our citizen?

The conversation usually starts with, 'who is the customer?' Where the best way to understand demand is by geography or 'fabric' then it is a pointless question anyway. If it is a personal demand and we are a problem for someone, then the word 'customer' could still be problematic. The word 'customer' implies the recipient of a product or service. It implies that the person is a 'consumer' and the other party is a provider. The relationship is clear: the provider has exclusive responsibility for provision and the consumer will be left to judge value for money. No one would question this in a commercial environment but should this be the relationship a public agency has with its citizens?

The consumer relationship leads to some unhealthy behaviour on both sides. The consumer can only really judge a service on value for money which means that they will become more and more demanding; 'I pay for the service, where is it? Why doesn't it work? Why can't they do it more often?' It means also that they will abdicate responsiblity and hand it to the professionals. 'My child has special needs, what are they doing about it?' It can seem from this perspective that parents do not bring children up these days, therapists and special needs coordinators do. The author of *The Abundant Community*, John McKnight, quotes a nice example; he tells of arriving at a youth centre where the walls were covered with flyers for activities. The kids were sitting around in varying stages of lethargy. He asked them what was wrong and they said, 'we're bored'. Even the kids have got used to being consumers where it is everyone else's job to entertain them.

Dependency on professionals

The behaviour on the delivery side is that services end up in the hands of the 'professional' who progresses by taking exams, getting qualifications and complying with standards. As the consumer becomes more demanding the main recourse to poor service is to become litigious – 'I did not get what I paid for'. The profession then has to protect itself until the apparent purpose is to 'be safe'. We do not allow children to be fostered because the system is obsessed with protecting itself – it strives to be safe, not to 'do things safely'. The police response to citizens trying to protect their communities during the 2011 riots was 'get these vigilantes off the streets, they are getting in our way'.

There is only one direction of travel for this logic – the citizen does less and less and the professional does more and more. The professional also has to invest more and more in standards, qualifications, training and legal protection. It can only lead to spiralling costs and ever poorer service and service perception.

What matters?

So, where to start? Managers in all public agencies need to start by learning what matters to citizens and communities. How would they describe what matters, what problems they are trying to solve? 'I can't control my kids', 'we want more control over what gets built here', 'we want an interest in what is developed here', 'we want facilities that work for us', 'we want to be able to look after our friends and neighbours', 'you keep telling me I'm a problem but you've never tried to help me', 'this place is so run down, it attracts all the worst people', and so on. None of these problems will be 'agency-shaped'. None will be the precise remit of the police, education, health, fire and rescue or local authority. Therefore, the most valuable place to start is 'in the work'. You can then use what you learn to engage the other agencies in a task of sharing knowledge and seeking to develop a common language that best describes 'what matters' in your geography.

Demand is the lever. It will take you away from sterile meetings where we worry about 'how to work together', all knowing that our respective measures and targets make it very difficult to cooperate. Learn how to solve the right problems together instead. The first step must be to reach shared knowledge of demand.

About the author

Richard Davis
Organisational Psychologist and Consultant at Vanguard
Tel: 01280 822255
Email: richard@vanguardconsult.co.uk

Richard has been a consultant with Vanguard for 20 years. He is an occupational psychologist by training. He started work in the Air Transport training board as a researcher developing job information systems with British Airways, BCAL and others. He was UK training manager for Avis before he joined Vanguard. He has worked in service organisations in both the private, public and third sectors.

10. SHARED SERVICES: A NO BRAINER?

John Seddon, Vanguard Consulting

Introduction

One of the key messages from the case studies in Part 1 and the previous chapter is that every system has a point of leverage. In most cases that point of leverage is 'demand'. You will see that demand can be treated in two ways.

The first way is to understand demand by learning what matters and by looking end-to-end to understand how to truly solve the problems you learn about – it is characterised by knowledge, relationships and the economy of flow.

The other view, the subject of this chapter, is the mass production logic where demand is treated as a transaction. It is then standardised to become a commodity and the task for ever after is to find cheaper ways of producing that commodity.

It is this logic that has led managers and ministers to think that shared services are a no brainer.

It seems obvious. If there are six organisations in the same field and each has an HR function, they should share the service and cut their costs. The amount of work would of course stay the same, but passing it through one organisation rather than six would require fewer buildings, managers, IT systems, suppliers and so on. Hence the notion that sharing services provides 'no brainer' opportunities for cutting costs.

Central costs such as HR and administration are conventionally allocated to operations, where the work is actually done. If these overheads are lower, transaction costs for the operations units must be lower too. To managers that makes sense, and it fits with another generally accepted view, the assumption that transaction costs are their most important concern. This is why shared-services managers and consultants put so much emphasis on the relative virtues of 'channels': telephone transactions being 'cheaper' than face-to-face ones, internet transactions 'cheaper' than telephone ones.

The culminating piece in the logic of this kind of shared service-design is an IT system to link the front- and back-office, enable the channels, allow managers to control the activity of the workforce and facilitate the processing of work.

Three basic arguments

These ideas constitute the three basic arguments for conventional shared services. The first two – which we might sum up respectively as 'less of a common resource' and 'efficiency through lower transaction costs' – originated in the economics literature. The third – IT as the enabler – is, of course, promoted by IT providers and scale consultancies.

The first is palpably obvious: achieving the same output from less of a given resource reduces cost. Many shared-services projects are based on these kinds of savings alone. But such savings are not always easy to achieve in practice and anyway relatively small.

As an example, take IT. Consolidating IT is a common source of anticipated savings in shared-services projects. But as examples in this book show, an IT system may not be needed in the first place, and the features of systems typically procured by local authorities and housing services actually serve to increase the costs and worsen the quality of service. It is spurious to claim savings in one place when, as a result, costs are incurred somewhere else. Can vacated buildings be sold? What are the costs associated with reducing managerial headcount?

Even shared-service protagonists concede that less-of-a-common-resource savings are marginal. They make much higher claims for the second strand – improved efficiency through lower transaction costs. As well as lowered transaction costs (higher volumes of work achieved by the same infrastructure, cheaper channels), they promise efficiency gains through staff specialisation and work standardisation– 'front offices' to handle telephone calls and 'back offices' to actually process the work. The rallying cry is 'simplify, standardise and then centralise', using an IT 'solution' as the means.

On paper, this all seems to make sense. But how does it square with the evidence? The fact is that we are witnessing a mounting series of embarrassing and costly shared-service failures.

Some, as in Western Australia, are a write-off from the start; they never get off the ground[11]. Many, like the UK Research Councils, have enormous teething problems, causing headaches for service users, who can't get the service they want, and suppliers, who can't get paid[12]. Most, as with the Department for Transport, run massively over budget[13]. And when managers try to undo the deal, like the Somerset councillors attempting to get out of their South West One shared service centre, they discover that disengagement is prohibitively expensive. Western Australia, just one of many failures down under, had to take the full cost of disengaging, an eye-watering AUS$90 million, on top of its failed investment of AUS$401 million[14].

Leaders in the public sector are all too often unaware that similar expensive failures have been racked up in the private sector. The difference, of course, is that private-sector leaders take care not to parade their dirty washing in public. The private sector was initially sold shared services by the same economists and 'scale' consultants who now pepper official propaganda with projected savings from other ventures as grist to the mill – as when Western Australia's projected savings were published in a Scottish Executive report extolling the virtues of sharing services!

It doesn't help that civil servants take 'evidence' from such sources without validating it. They do so because policy is driven by ministers, and while 'evidence-based policy is sought by government … mostly the result is policy-based evidence'. If anything, ministers are pushing sharing services harder, even as the evidence of failure mounts. At the time of writing, the minister for the Cabinet Office has made it clear that services will be shared across central government departments; the

11 Western Australia's Department of Treasury and Finance Shared Service Centre (2011) promised savings of AUS$56 million, but incurred costs of AUS$401 million.

12 A National Audit Office report (2011) said that the UK Research Councils project was due to be completed by December 2009 at a cost of £79 million. But, in reality, it was not completed until March 2011, at a cost of £130 million.

13 The Department for Transport's Shared Services, initially forecast to save £57 million, is now estimated to cost the taxpayer £170 million, a failure in management that the House of Commons Public Accounts Committee described as a display of 'stupendous incompetence'. The most recent evidence of the higher cost was documented in a House of Commons Transport Select Committee report (2010).

14 See http://yhoo.it/uVMIZH (accessed 13/2/12)

Cabinet Office has even established a framework agreement to enable departments to purchase the service directly, without the trauma of tendering. Like many others, ministers believe in economies of scale and 'digital by default'. Alas, they have been led astray by a common bias: as John Kay (2012) has also noted, 'Our intuitions about the merits of centralisation and scale are generally wrong'.

Most large-scale IT projects fail

Before I explain why bigger isn't cheaper, it should be pointed out that the evidence is that the vast majority of large-scale IT projects fail: something the IT industry doesn't talk about but that every manager, and minister for that matter, ought to know. In their aptly-titled book, *Dangerous Enthusiasms*, Gauld and Goldfinch (2006) provide a veritable tsunami of evidence to show that as many as 30% of IT projects fail completely while a further 60% go far over budget and/or fail to meet specifications. Western Australia is an example of the former, while the Department of Transport and UK Research Councils are examples of the latter.

The high rate of IT investment failure should be enough on its own to create a presumption against IT-driven change. But even when shared-service ventures are implemented according to plan, they create costs in a more insidious way.

Managing costs causes costs

Paradoxically, focusing on lowering transaction costs actually drives costs up. An early example of this phenomenon occurred when local authorities were set a target to establish call centres by April 2005. When consultants were hired to help them move 'telephone work' over from council departments, call volumes shot up. Why? The increase in call volumes was all 'failure demand' (Seddon 2003) – demand caused by a failure to do something or do something right for the customer. The assumption that telephone work can be usefully separated from service provision is a classic case of misplaced faith in scale and centralisation; as a direct result, call centres were stuffed with progress-chasing of various forms as people tried to put the two together again. Installing IT systems for what was called 'customer relationship management' (CRM) only served to institutionalise the waste.

Unfortunately, management's focus on transaction costs, fostered by the 'scale' consultancies, blinded it to the fact that while transaction costs were indeed lower, transaction numbers were inexorably rising as their system failed to provide service that worked for the customer. One reaction to increasing call volumes was (and is) to add more resource – hire more people to pick up the phones – which of course nullifies any gain from lower transaction costs. Another is to outsource call-handling to lower wage economies, ignoring the fact that contracts are commonly priced according to transaction volumes. Being paid by volume, outsource providers have no incentive to tackle high levels of failure demand, whose costs are thus locked in for the term of the contract.

Many authorities are trying to move services to the web – 'digital by default' being the mantra – only to learn what they could have learned from their call centre experience: focusing on costs leads to a failure to focus on value, creating large amounts of waste in the form of failure demand.

We return to focusing on value shortly. But first we need to examine how back offices have also driven costs up. The idea of the back office was first mooted by Richard Chase (1978). He started from the premise that the job of a service manager was to maximise the use of resources, which in services consist largely of people. He observed that the customers often 'interfered' with the management process, interrupting work and preventing staff from working productively. So, to maximise productivity, he proposed splitting the work between a front office, where customers' needs would be documented in some fashion (usually involving IT), and a back office, where labour could now be optimised without interruption. In this logic the back office provided a further opportunity for increasing productivity by standardising work and specialising the workforce, leading to reductions in operating and training costs.

Examination of what actually happens in such IT-dominated industrial designs reveals massive disruptions to the service flow; for the customer, service is anything but smooth. There is huge waste in the shape of hand-offs, rework, duplication of effort, and a focus on meeting activity targets and service levels. All these 'system conditions' lengthen the time it takes to deliver a service and consequently create failure demand. In other words, the service gets worse and the total cost of service goes up. On all counts such industrial designs fail miserably.

The most egregious example of this failure is Her Majesty's Revenue and Customs (HMRC) (whose amalgamation by Gordon Brown is another example of official obsession with scale and centralisation). HMRC has gone lean and gone wrong. It is a classic instance of service industrialisation, based on the belief that taxation can be mass-produced as in manufacturing. The work has been standardised and specialised. The management focus is on activity, not purpose. In a misguided attempt to create a performance culture, workers are set to solving management's wrong problem – why didn't we meet our targets yesterday?

While HMRC managers assure House of Commons select committees that lower transaction costs will bring improvements, the evidence is of mounting failure demand. Accountants have built web sites to complain about the number of transactions it takes to get a service. Even when callers to HMRC's call centres can get through they are left uncertain about the advice they have received. AdviceUK, the umbrella for welfare advice organisations, has established that it is costing member organisations across the country at least £500 million to mop up failure demand downstream from HMRC and the equally dysfunctional Department of Work and Pensions (DWP).

Shared-service ventures fail because they are based on 'industrial' designs featuring IT-led service factories that promise economies of scale. Scale thinkers mistakenly think that the fact that some channels are inherently cheaper than others is more important than the design of the service, thus unwittingly causing failure demand. They are equally wrong in assuming that lower transaction costs will lead to improvement, when the total number of transactions it takes customers to get a service is rising. Based on the central idea that costs are associated with activity, service managers bear down on exactly the wrong lever and drive their costs up.

Managing value drives costs out

Yes, some channels are indeed cheaper than others – but which channels can work for which services? Booking a squash court works online if the website is designed from the user's point of view. Most public services are infinitely more complex than that. Yet children's services, adult social care, housing benefits and planning (development control) have all been moved to industrial shared-service designs, with disastrous consequences.

Computer systems are simply not flexible enough to absorb the variety and complexity of demand faced by most public services. People, and only people, are. With a thorough understanding of demand from the customer's point of view, the human expertise required to serve that demand is created at the point of transaction. All of the case studies in this book illustrate this basic principle. All employ measures that relate to the purpose of the service from the customer's point of view, and these measures are used where the work is done to understand and improve service delivery. Working this way focuses on managing value, not cost. Another paradox: focusing on value drives costs out.

The better way to share services

To return to our six organisations and their HR functions: the first step in sharing services is to study the service where it is, and the second to improve it, again *in situ*. In cases where this has been done, HR productivity has as much as doubled (Middleton 2010). For IT help-desks, productivity has risen by 20% while service has improved (Middleton 2010). These examples, like the cases spelled out in this book, illustrate the counter-intuitive truth that true economy comes from flow, not scale. Having achieved significant improvement, managers can then, and only then, consider whether further economies can be achieved by using less of a common resource – the third and final step.

Compared to conventional IT-led industrial shared-service attempts, this better approach avoids all the risks associated with planned change; indeed, the risks are eliminated through the first step – developing knowledge – and subsequently using that knowledge to improve. Those improvements are realised in months.

Careful study of industrialised shared-service designs reveals the important truth that industrialisation itself is the flaw. What becomes immediately apparent is that standardised, IT-driven factory processes are incapable of absorbing the variety of customer demand, making it a struggle for customers to get what they want. When customers can't get what they want (especially in public services where there is no alternative) they return until they do. Failure demand of this kind represents a massive hidden cost. It can run as high as 80% of all customer demand in industrialised shared-services projects, locking in costs for many years.

Understanding this and other problems with industrialisation leads to a better approach: placing the (human) expertise required to solve people's problems at the place where they meet the service provider, usually locally. Instead of being processed by demoralised and disengaged workers in remote computer-controlled factories, citizen needs are understood and acted on by enthusiastic, helpful people who are motivated by providing a service that both matters and works. Overall costs tumble because citizens need fewer transactions to get a service, irrespective of channel. Ironically, this is a lesson that *does* come from manufacturing. It was first learned by Taiichi Ohno, the architect of the Toyota Production System, in the 1950s: that the economies that matter are achieved through flow, not scale.

References

Chase, R.B., 1978, 'Where does the customer fit in a service operation?' *Harvard Business Review*, Vol. 56 No. 4, pp. 137-42

Gauld, R. and Goldfinch, S., 2006. *Dangerous Enthusiasms.* *E-government, Computer Failure and Information System Development* Otago University Press: New Zealand

House of Commons Transport Committee 2010, 'The performance of the Department for Transport: Government response to the Committee's Fourth Report of Session 2009–10' Third Special Report of Session 2010–11 House of Commons, London: HM Stationery Office. See http:// bit.ly/HK2IOZ (accessed 13/2/12)

Kay, J. 'Darwin's marriage and war in Iraq: the missing link', *Financial Times* 14 May 2008, p13

Kay, J. 'A real market economy ensures that greed is good', *Financial Times* 18 January 2012

Middleton, P. (2010), *Delivering Public Services that Work (Volume 1):* Triarchy Press: Axminster

National Audit Office 2011'Shared services in the Research Councils: Report by the Comptroller and Auditor General' Department for

Business, Innovation and Skills HC 1459 HC 1459 Session 2010–2012. See http://bit.ly/o4AnOa (accessed 13/2/12)

Seddon, J. 2003, *Freedom from Command and Control*, Vanguard Consulting Ltd: Buckingham.

'Failed OSS plan will swallow extra $90m' December 15th *The West Australian* 2011. See http://yhoo.it/uVMIZH

Western Australia Economic Regulation Authority 2011 'Inquiry into the Benefits and Costs Associated with the Provision of Shared Corporate Services in the Public Sector- Final Report', Perth ,WA. See http://bit.ly/pa46bl for more details (accessed 13/2/12)

AFTERWORD

IT'S CHEAPER TO DO IT PROPERLY

Charlotte Pell, Vanguard Consulting

The purpose of this chapter is to illustrate with fictional stories from the public, the surprising truth that it's cheaper to do it properly. You might find these stories worthy, mundane, repetitive or even familiar. This is because they are. We are all worthy of proper help from public services when we need it. The stories are repetitive because public sector managers repeat the same mistakes. The stories are familiar because we have all experienced poor service and mundane because public services tend to deal with everyday life. I've given the people in the stories names because people do have names. Each story relates to a case study in Part 1 of this book.

Mr and Mrs Dawson's microwave caught fire. They saw an advert for free fire home checks and made an appointment. They thought the woman who came round was lovely but she spent more time filling in a form than she did helping them. Instead of talking to them normally, she seemed to be reading off a script. They were left with a folder full of leaflets and a copy of the form arrived in the post a week later. But the couple felt so overwhelmed by information, they never got round to doing anything. Mrs Dawson got a customer satisfaction survey in the post a few months later. She remembered how nice the woman was and ticked 'Excellent' for everything.

Sue saw a box of raw chickens on a sunny window sill in the kitchen of a local restaurant. She rang the council to tell them. She thought she was doing the right thing. Instead of a thank you, she was put through to Customer Services who asked her a series of questions, none of which related to the chickens. She had three follow-up phone calls, the first to ask her what she thought should be done, the second to tell her something was being done and the third to ask her if she was satisfied with how her call had been handled. She also received two incomprehensible letters that went straight in the bin. As she explained when she first called, she just wanted to report it. She expected the council would do something about it but instead of a thank you, she was dogged by correspondence. She was surprised by all the attention because she thought the council was short of money.

Joan had her third stroke on Boxing Day. The ambulance took her straight to A&E where she spent 2½ hours in a medical assessment unit. She was seen by five different people who put needles in her hand. She finally got to the Acute Stroke Unit where she spent 15 days. Her daughter, Pearl, felt she had to fight to get her mum looked after. She thought staff had written her off because she was old and frail. No one asked Pearl what her mum was like before the stroke. In fact, no one seemed to be doing anything. Pearl was surprised to see a tick in a box next to 'relatives informed of patient's condition and progress' in a document at the bottom of her mother's bed.

Fred was pleased to show off his new kitchen to the inspector when she came to inspect his restaurant for the second time. Instead of being impressed, she sent him a threatening letter telling him they would close him down. He had no idea what he was doing wrong. It didn't help that his son, who helped him understand his correspondence, was away when the first letter came. Fred couldn't believe they were talking about his restaurant when his son read out the words 'failure' and 'offence' because he had never failed at anything. The inspectors had been so friendly when they visited the first time. His restaurant was his life and he would do anything to keep it open. He didn't understand why they wanted to shut him down.

Mr Kowalski wanted to build an extension to his shop. He asked for help with his application but instead of giving him help, the receptionist pointed him to a wall of leaflets. He was told it would take up to eight weeks to get a decision. After seven weeks, he got a letter saying the application had errors in it. He was invited to correct the errors and submit another one for free. He rang the call centre for help but instead of helping, they told him he would get a phone call within 48 hours. No one rang so he went to the Town Hall. They told him to return after 3.30pm. When he returned, no one was available. Mr Kowalski submitted a complaint and stopped work on his application. He was surprised no one was available to help him in the first place. He thought the council wanted to see businesses do well.

Ryan was being bullied in his new care home. He was too scared to ask for help and felt the only solution was to run away. The care home had no choice but to report him as a missing person because workers didn't have time to go out and look for him. It was the eleventh time he'd run away and the police found him each time and brought him back. When he returned, his care worker would tell him off for wasting police time. No one asked him what was wrong. He was surprised no one noticed how unhappy he was.

Where would you start?

If you were the manager of one of the services above, where would you start to put things right? Perhaps you would put your faith in an initiative that promises to help you place greater emphasis on the customer, such as Personalisation, Putting People First, Customer First, Customer Insight, People First Commissioning, Citizen First or Patient Choice.

Or would you place your bet on changing one big thing? Imagine if there was a lever, that if only you could find it and pull it, everything would start to improve. Would you pull:

- The people lever (train or coach your staff)?

- The structure lever (rename departments; move people around)?

- The IT lever (buy or improve your IT)?

- The control lever (more standards and specifications from above)?

- The governance lever (change the way the organisation is led)?

- The chief executive lever (train your chief executive or swap them for another one)?

- The procurement lever (buy stuff better)?

- The marketing lever (tell people things have got better)?

- The culture lever (change the way things are done around here)?

- The ownership lever (transfer delivery of the service to an outside organsiation)?

- The process lever (isolate and improve processes)?

How much time and money would you spend on finding out which one made a difference? And how would you know?

Whichever lever you choose, it is likely to involve a plan.

The managers in this book started with none of the levers above. They decided not to take a leap of faith by gambling on a plan, committing to an untested initiative or a copying a solution to someone else's problem. Instead, they took a scientific approach; they got data.

The biggest lever

The managers in this book chose to pull the demand lever. When you pull the demand lever, you get knowledge about how things really are. That's not 'Get Knowledge' with a capital G and K. The practical action taken by the authors of this book didn't need capital letters, a logo or its own special name. They did what they needed to, in their own service, to find out what was really going on for customers. They devoted time and attention to analysing in great detail why people were coming in or ringing, what people really needed and what really mattered to them. In some cases this meant listening to a few hundred phone calls over a period of weeks. In one case, managers studied over 20,000 demands from callers and visitors across a large geographical area.

To find out more about how to understand demand, go back to Chapter 9.

You learn that the system is in charge

When you study how your organisation responds to demand, you find all sorts of strange things. To return to our stories, managers found the system rang Sue when she didn't want a call. It sent Fred a letter when he would have preferred a conversation. It didn't treat Joan as a human being and let Ryan down badly when he needed help. It gave Mr Kowalski the run-around and punished Fred for doing his best. It gave Mr and Mrs Dawson an hour with a smart young woman. But it did nothing to prevent a fire.

What is this 'it' that does the strange things? We have all experienced it. It runs much of the public sector. It spews out the wrong letters to the wrong people. It gets the amounts we are owed wrong. It does things in 48 hours. It doesn't do things in 48 hours. It generates letters we don't understand. It is inflexible. It can only deal with one part of our query at a time. It doesn't listen or understand. It certainly doesn't care. It can only go in one direction and at a certain speed. It doesn't recognise anything outside its boxes. It comes in piles of paper six inches thick. It tells us we are third in the queue. It threatens us out of the blue. It is very sorry. It gives us a unique customer reference number. It tells us our session has timed out. It takes a very long time. It makes us angry and lets us down.

But 'it' cannot deal with variety. It makes life difficult and wastes public money.

Doing it properly

When Food Safety Officers at Great Yarmouth listened to the concerned citizens who reported dodgy practice in restaurants, they learnt that most people trust the council to do something. Like Sue, they don't need phone calls and letters. It's cheaper to give people what they need and no more.

When ward staff at Plymouth Hospital studied four years of data, they learnt that frail patients who'd had a stroke before, like Joan, need special attention to get them back on their feet and out of hospital. Treating every patient as if they are the same might meet national standards but it didn't help Joan. It's expensive to keep someone in a hospital bed for two weeks. Ward staff learnt it's cheaper to understand people before you treat them.

Fred is a good businessman. He runs a popular restaurant but he doesn't know how to clean a kitchen thoroughly. Food inspectors learnt it was quicker to show him how to clean than to send him a threatening letter and serve a notice on him. It's cheaper to assume people want to do the right thing. Most of the time they do and if it turns out they don't want to, you are more likely to find this out by listening to them.

Filling in forms doesn't prevent house fires. Mr and Mrs Dawson wanted advice on preventing a fire in their own home with its unique combination of wiring, appliances and layout. They wanted the friendly woman to listen to their concerns and give them advice. Instead it was a wasted visit. It was costing the fire service a lot of money to do the wrong thing.

If Mr Kowalski had been allowed to see a planning officer (and the eight week target didn't exist), his first application would have been good enough. It could have been processed in days. Keeping him away from the experts ended up costing the council more staff time in logging, tracking, sending out letters and complaint handling. It also delayed what would have been an excellent development and a boost to the town. It would have been better and cheaper to do it properly the first time around.

On the twelfth time Ryan ran away, the police officer came with Ryan into the care home. Instead of dashing off, she had a coffee with his carer. Ryan was worried. They were in a room for ages. He didn't want them to talk to each other because he'd told them different lies. He needn't have worried because his carer came to sit with him and was genuinely concerned. Ryan admitted he wasn't happy and after two weeks of conversations, he told the truth about the bullying. Soon after, he was moved back to his old care home where he had nothing to run away from. He was safe. In this case, it was cheaper for the police officer and care worker to understand what was really going on. All Ryan needed was a good listening to.

Put staff back in charge

These kinds of cases are not unusual. They show that public services serve people with a variety of needs and circumstances.

So, what can deal with variety? What can deal with people with a variety of needs? What can deal with people who express their needs differently? What can understand context? What can adapt to different speeds and take things in a different order? What can we develop a relationship with? What can see the bigger picture? What can react quickly, listen, reassure and explain? What can make decisions and judgements quickly? What can learn? What can tell when we're lying? What can connect with us?

The answer isn't a what. It's a who. The answer is a human being. Only a human being can deal with the variety of needs and circumstances involved when people go missing or have a stroke. But not just any human being – and certainly not a robot; – it must be someone who has the authority and expertise to understand what is going on and to treat customers as human beings, not as individual transactions.

Sue, Joan and her family, Fred, Mr and Mrs Dawson, Mr Kowalski, Ryan and John didn't get what they needed because of the design of the system. The staff had not been given the flexibility or authority to do the right thing. Instead, they were locked into doing stupid things that wasted money. When the same people were put back in charge, this all changed; they were able to do what mattered to the customer.

The big surprise

The biggest surprise for many people is that it is cheaper to do it properly. It's counter-intuitive to managers to let people see a planning or benefits expert immediately. It's counter-intuitive to pay a lot of attention to frail stroke patients when they first come through the door. It's counter-intuitive to listen to proud restaurant owners and concerned homeowners instead of getting on with the serious work of ticking boxes and sending out letters. It's counter-intuitive to understand 'difficult' people instead of punishing them.

When you study your system, you start to see things very differently. You begin to see what really costs money. You see that it costs staff time to answer phone calls from the same people because they didn't get help the first time around, to write and send out letters that no one reads, to do things eight times instead of once, correct errors, deal with complaints and feed IT systems that give nothing back. It costs even more when people end up in hospital or in court because of an initial failure in the system.

Understanding demand leads you to discover the mundane, everyday details of people's lives, their needs and their problems — things which are not normally attractive to managers who prefer the 'strategic' business of meetings and reports. But most managers find that discovering how their organisation really performs is life changing. Often, for the first time in many years, managers remember why they decided to work in the public sector and professionals get to do the job they were trained to do. Politicians, civil servants, policy makers and journalists get excited because, although they don't understand how it happened, they see much better service, happier staff and lower costs.

Improving service has halved the cost of stroke care in Plymouth, released officers to deal with serious offences in Wolverhampton, saved Rugby Borough Council's planning service £168,000, significantly increased the number of businesses in Great Yarmouth producing safe food, reduced an enormous administrative burden on Staffordshire Fire and Rescue, halved the cost of advice cases in Nottingham, prevented unnecessary, unhelpful and expensive hospital treatment for vulnerable adults in Somerset and reduced the number of missing persons reports, currently costing Cheshire Police £3.8 million, by an incredible 75%. The savings to the wider public and the social benefits of these interventions are far greater than this.

Every public sector manager has the opportunity to make massive savings and improvements in service by ending the reign of clipboards, letters, call centre scripts, forms and targets. If you don't know where to start, don't take a leap of faith and gamble on a plan. Instead, take a 'leap of fact', study your own system, get knowledge and do it properly.

GLOSSARY

Capability Chart: Significantly more powerful than most management information tools. Records performance over time and analyses the variation in the results. It indicates if a process is in or out of control.

Check: This is the process of creating the knowledge of how an organisation is actually working from a customer's perspective.

Clean: ensuring all the information needed to resolve the issue is available.

Command and control: This is the dominant management model in the public sector. It does work but is inherently wasteful. It emphasises a top-down, hierarchical approach with a focus on targets, standards and budgets.

Commodity: A product or service treated as a simple transaction. The view is that it has little function beyond its face value. Anyone can make it and it serves a simple purpose so you can buy it in bulk. For example, a blood test could be thought of as a commodity but if you think about it properly it is part of a diagnostic process, i.e. a problem-solving activity. When you think about it in this way, you can see that 80% of blood tests are waste/unnecessary and just done to tick a box. If the doctor does not know the patient then they don't know what to test for, so they test for everything.

Common cause variation: Variation attributable to the normal running of the system. The causes are systemic and predictable and 'designed in'.

Demand, nature of: Customer demand is generally much more consistent and predictable than is perceived. Therefore assembling precise data on the real nature of demand is invaluable for designing better processes.

Demand, designing against: 'Against' in this context means to design the service in anticipation of demand in order to be able to meet it.

End-to-end time: This is a measure of the total time the service took as experienced by the customer. As conventional metrics are of activity within functional management silos, the total time the customer experiences is often not known. This metric often indicates waste and poor performance levels.

Failure demand: Demand caused by a failure to do something or to do something right for the customer.

Flow: Understanding the precise path the work takes through your organisation is vital. Unnecessary specialisation of staff often causes the route the work follows to become convoluted. Tracking the work often reveals unnecessary stages, rework and delays.

Hand-offs: Command and control managers believe that specialised units are more effective. But fragmenting the way work is handled requires it to be passed between the specialists. This transferring is an overhead which causes wasteful rework and reduces job satisfaction. Hand-offs should therefore be kept to a minimum.

Intervention: Engaging with an organisation to help it to improve its performance. The task is to help people learn to see their work differently so they can be more effective managers.

Job 1: The day job.

Job 2: Improvement activity.

Management by colours: e.g. 'red' and 'green'. Conventional management reports often use traffic lights or blobs in an attempt to show whether something is getting better or worse. However, comparing one number with another number and adding a colour tells you nothing about the true performance of the system.

Measures: In command and control organisations measures are top down and focus on budgets, targets and standards. Better measures are integrated with the work and focus on capability and variation. They are empowering for the workforce rather than a mechanism for control and compliance. A key distinction is that 'command and control' measures are typically arbitrary; systems measures are always real.

Nominal Value: Taguchi's observation that by first understanding exactly what a customer wants we can then aim at perfection. This is significantly better than working to tolerances or a range of performance.

Outside-in: An understanding of an organisation from outside the organisation, e.g. an understanding from the customer perspective. This perspective is diametrically opposed to an 'inside out' perspective.

Predictable demand: demand is usually remarkably consistent. By capturing the data to demonstrate this, process redesign is made much simpler and more effective.

Preventable demand: if the system was able to do only and exactly what was needed the first time/once then this demand would be prevented.

Purpose: This must be defined in customer terms for a coherent and aligned organisation. Commonly organisations work to a *de facto* purpose such as 'make the budget' or 'meet the target'. This is dysfunctional as people's efforts and ingenuity become focused on the *de facto* purpose rather than the customer.

Redesign phase: Once the purpose, profile of demand and the true capability of the organisation to service this demand have been understood, then experiments can take place to work out how to improve. The organisation can then be redesigned using this new knowledge.

Rework: If a process is fragmented then oversight can be lost and different stages will inadvertently make work for, and inflict costs on, each other. This is common where organisations are sub-optimised into specialist functional units.

Roll-in: A method to scale up a change to the whole organisation that was successful in one area. Change is not imposed. Instead each area needs to learn how to do the analysis of waste for themselves and devise their own solutions. This approach engages the workforce and produces better, more sustainable solutions. Compare to 'roll-out'.

Roll-out: Method that involves developing an improved process, standardising it and applying it to other areas. This tends to create two problems: first, the solution is not optimised for each specific context so is not a good fit; secondly, the staff in the other teams have not been through the same learning and therefore feel little sense of ownership. They may also feel a loss of control and resist change.

Silo: The practice of organising workers into separate functional hierarchies. Each silo tends to work to optimise its own performance, but the result is a damaging sub-optimisation overall.

Special cause variation: Unpredictable variation attributable to a specific event.

System archetype: An archetype is a typical model or type on which other similar things are patterned. A system archetype might be a 'break-fix' system like an IT Helpdesk or a Housing Repairs system. Identifying a system archetype may help you locate the most appropriate lever for change.

System conditions: The causes of waste. These are the measures, targets, inspection regimes or rewards that influence how a system performs. Others include: IT systems, management behaviour, organisational structures, rules and procedures. Understanding these is critical. For example, a target that all emails must be replied to within 24 hours may well result in busy people sending 'random' replies to meet the target. Unless this system condition is removed, and the underlying issues addressed, limited improvement will be possible. The vital point is that you need to understand the key system conditions in any particular flow.

Targets: In a conventional command and control hierarchy, targets tend to refer to arbitrary numerical goals. The key attribute of a target is that managers use them to manage people.

Transaction: A single transfer of goods or services.

Value demand: This is demand that you *do* want. This comes from customers who are requesting new services and updating their accounts. It is the reason the organisation exists.

Waste: Any activity that does not add value to the customer.

Work, in the: physically in the flow of the value work - you only know what you see not what you are told.

Working to purpose: being mindful at all times as to the purpose of the system and ensuring that all work is consistent with that purpose.

About John Seddon

John Seddon trained as an occupational psychologist and is known around the world for his pioneering work on change in public and private sector organisations. He translated and adapted the Toyota Production System into a methodology called The Vanguard Method for use by service organisations.

He is also known as an informed and controversial critic of both management fads and much of the theory that underpins public sector reform.

He is Managing Director of Vanguard Ltd, a consultancy that helps service organisations change from a command-and-control design to a systems design, a Visiting Professor at Derby and Hull universities and a fellow of the public policy think-tank ResPublica.

About Charlotte Pell

Charlotte started her career in local government as a Community Development Worker. A decade of promotions into less useful jobs with more senior titles taught her that doing the right thing for the citizen is more important than a career with employers who rewarded her for compliance. This led her to leave local government in pursuit of a more practical job in the voluntary sector. Here she started to follow John Seddon's work.

Charlotte now works for Vanguard Consulting and her job is to generate curiosity about the Vanguard Method among public sector managers who are unhappy with the prevailing style of management.

Related Titles and Authors from Triarchy Press

(visit www.triarchypress.com/SystemsThinking for a full list of titles)

The Vanguard Method

Systems Thinking in the Public Sector - *John Seddon*

Delivering Public Services that Work Volume 1 - *Peter Middleton*

The Need for Change - *Stuart Corrigan*

Other Systems Thinking titles

Systems Thinking for Curious Managers - With 40 new Management f-LAWS - *Russell Ackoff*

This book includes an insightful, extended introduction to Systems Thinking as developed by Russ Ackoff.

Managers as Designers in The Public Services: Beyond Technomagic - *David Wastell*

Professor Wastell's revealing explanation of why the public sector keeps turning to large-scale IT 'solutions' - and keeps being disappointed. He uses detailed case studies to present a workable way for public sector managers to design their way out of problems rather than imposing monolithic solutions. This is a book about Systems Thinking and Design Thinking in practice.

The Search for Leadership: An Organisational Perspective -
William Tate

This Systems Thinking approach to leadership asks us to look beyond individuals, managers, leaders and management training programmes. It reviews a range of issues like: distributing authority ~ management vs. organisation development ~ structural gaps that account for waste, rework, poor communication and failure ~ transferring learning ~ organisational competence ~ accountability ~ the organisation's culture and shadow-side.

www.triarchypress.com